HANDBOOK OF BUSINESS QUOTATIONS

HANDBOOK OF BUSINESS QUOTATIONS

Compiled by
George Thomas Kurian

Prentice-Hall, Inc., Englewood Cliffs, New Jersey

Prentice-Hall International, Inc., *London*
Prentice-Hall of Australia, Pty. Ltd., *Sydney*
Prentice-Hall Canada, Inc., *Toronto*
Prentice-Hall of India Private Ltd., *New Delhi*
Prentice-Hall of Japan, Inc., *Tokyo*
Prentice-Hall of Southeast Asia Pte. Ltd., *Singapore*
Editora Prentice-Hall do Brasil Ltda., *Rio de Janeiro*
Prentice-Hall Hispanoamericana, S.A., *Mexico*

Library of Congress Cataloging-in-Publication Data

Handbook of business quotations.

Includes index.
  1. Business—Quotations, maxims, etc.
2. Businessmen—Quotations. I. Kurian,
George Thomas.
PN6084.B87H36 1987   081   86-30530

ISBN 0-13-376500-8

Printed in the United States of America

FOREWORD

Handbook of Business Quotations is a carefully selected and blended potpourri of quotations dealing with almost all areas of contemporary business. Some are practical rules of thumb while others are nuggets of corporate wisdom; some shine with the patina of tradition while others are as sharp as a scalpel; some are sage exhortations while others are reflections of long business careers recollected in tranquillity; some are warnings and admonitions while others are moral imperatives couched in evangelical language; some are plain folk maxims, while others are just socko humor.

Handbook of Business Quotations is a unique compilation because, unlike other books of quotations, it contains only quotations on business, for business, and by businesspeople. These quotations reveal the business mind at work—its texture, its strengths, its hopes, its weaknesses, its motivations, its fears, and its faults. How do businesspeople perceive themselves? What are their recipes for success? What are their favorite philosophies and creeds? What are their attitudes toward the non-business world around them? The answers contain few surprises. The quotations show that the vast majority of businesspeople are solid citizens, heavily conservative, with a solid deposit of Calvinist virtues of hard work and thrift. They are patriotic to a fault and proud of their work and their country. Their favorite words are profit and efficiency. They prefer the plain and earthy to the erudite and profound.

These quotations are designed to be used as tools in communication. They provide you with instant eloquence and also attest to the quality of your knowledge and the breadth of your experience. Use them also as anchors for ideas and pegs to hang them on. Use them often; most of them can stand a lot of wear and tear and never lose their freshness or sharpness through use. In fact, they get better with repetition.

The over 900 quotations in the book are grouped within more than 350 subject categories from accomplishment to zeal. The table of contents lists them in alphabetical order for instant reference. Many categories contain several quotations; for example, *Advertising* contains 30 quotes, *Money* 22, *Profit* 26, *Success* 19. There are also quotations on specific areas of business, such as banking and management.

The quotations cover not only a wide range of issues and subjects, but also a variety of target audiences. They are meant not only for the business speaker but also for the business writer and communicator. Specifically, they have been selected for use in the 11 most common business situations:

- **Sales Presentations**
  Look under: *Consumer Products, Creativity, Ideas, Markets.*
- **Conferences and Meetings**
  Look under: *Business Leadership, Management, Organization.*
- **Press Conferences**
  Look under: *Business Credibility, Golden Rule, Productivity.*
- **Memos and Internal Communications**
  Look under: *Committee, Credibility, Pessimism, Simplicity.*
- **As Fillers in Corporate Publications**
  Look under: *Corporate Responsibility, Forecasting, Size.*
- **New Product Introduction**
  Look under: *America, Facts, Invention, Pioneering.*
- **In Advertising and Sales Literature**
  Look under: *Advertising, Information, Standards, Thought.*
- **Awards Presentations**
  Look under: *Character, Efficiency, Sales, Success.*
- **Stockholders' Meetings**
  Look under: *Annual Meeting, Teamwork, Social Responsibility, Stewardship.*
- **Position Papers**
  Look under: *Ethics, Problem-Solving, Progress, Public Service.*
- **Counseling Employees**
  Look under: *Achievement, Confidence, Determination, Winning.*

No matter what the situation, *Handbook of Business Quotations* gives you a quote that fits the occasion and the audience. But it does more than that. These quotes can help to deliver a specific type of message in a specific format. For example, if you are looking for openers and closers that will stick like burrs to the memory of your salespeople, then consider the following:

- All business proceeds on belief or judgment or probability, and not on certainties. *Charles W. Eliot*
- A Company cannot increase productivity; people can. *Robert Half*
- When you see a successful business, someone once made a courageous decision. *Peter F. Drucker*

Or suppose you want to lighten your speech with humor, then try these lines:

- There are only two areas where new ideas are terribly dangerous— economics and sex. *Felix Rohatyn*
- The mark of a true executive is usually illegible. *Leo J. Farrell, Jr.*
- An economist is a man who makes the obvious incomprehensible. *Alfred A. Knopf*

If you want to light a fire under your listeners and readers with memorable pieces of inspiration and advice, consider the following:

- Paying attention to simple little things that most men neglect makes a few men rich. *Henry Ford*
- Success or failure in business is caused more by mental attitudes than by mental capacities. *Walter Dill Scott*
- I can give you a six-word formula for success: "Think things through, then follow through." *Edward Rickenbacker*
- Successful salesmanship (is) 90% preparation and 10% presentation. *B. R. Canfield*
- If you count *all* your assets, you *always* show a profit. *Robert Quillen*

If you want to astonish your listeners or readers with provocative and pithy definitions, then try the following:

- A committee is a cul de sac down which ideas are lured and then quietly strangled. *Barnett Cocks*
- Consultants are people who borrow your watch, tell you what time it is, and then walk off with the watch. *Robert Townsend*
- Finance is the art of passing currency from hand to hand until it finally disappears. *Robert W. Sarnoff*
- Power means not having to raise your voice. *George Will*

The catchment area of *Handbook of Business Quotations* is as broad as business itself, and so is the range of those quoted. From Charles F. Abbott to Darryl F. Zanuck, the galaxy of business greats is fully represented in this collection—515 names in all. For example; you'll be able to choose from quotes by Frank W. Woolworth, Andrew Carnegie, David Sarnoff, Alfred P. Sloan, J. Pierpont Morgan, Thomas Watson and hundreds more.

Look under the Name Index for a full list of names. They are among the most successful practitioners of American business ideas as well as the most successful Americans in the nation's history. They are also among the most quotable.

I would, in conclusion, like to express my gratitude to David Wright and Nancy Brandwein, editors at Prentice-Hall, for their patience, support, and many valuable suggestions, as well as their confidence in this project.

George Thomas Kurian

TABLE OF CONTENTS

HANDBOOK OF
BUSINESS
QUOTATIONS

A

ACCOMPLISHMENT

Too many of us, when we accomplish what we set out to do, exclaim "See what I have done," instead of saying, "See where I have been led."

Henry Ford

ACCOUNTABILITY

The chief executive of a large American corporation is today probably the most accountable executive of any institution in American society. Competition in labor, capital, and product markets compels him to account daily to his employees, stockholders, bankers, and customers. He is also accountable to society under a host of federal, state, and municipal laws.

Neil H. Jacoby

ACHIEVEMENT

It is amazing what ordinary people can do if they set out without preconceived notions.

Charles F. Kettering

ACTION

If there is quiet, it is necessary to do something. If there is protest, it is a sign of strength to give in to reasoned demands.

Ralf Dahrendorf

ADMEN

A good advertising man who is also a good businessman has an interesting edge over everyone. He works for a lot of clients, knows a little about a lot, and agile minds can transfer ideas from industry to industry like a bee hopping from plant to plant.

Andrew Kershaw

ADVERTISING

Advertisements contain the only truths to be relied on in a newspaper.

Thomas Jefferson

If advertising encourages people to live beyond their means, so does matrimony.

Bruce Barton

The best thing is recognizing that honesty sells. There is no reason why honesty cannot be combined with the skills of persuasion.

William Bernbach

Anybody can be a big hit in this business [advertising] if he meets two requirements. He has to have a new path and he has to be able to run fast down that path.

William Bernbach

The advertiser who thinks he thinks he has to choose between the straight-forward and dull or the beautiful but dumb is mistaken. The trick is to be relevant as well as bright.

William Bernbach

The business that considers itself immune to the necessity of advertising sooner or later finds itself immune to business.

Derby Brown

A revolution in advertising is already in motion. Consumer cynicism has already forced the advertiser toward humor, toward the underclaim, or no claim at all. But this in turn will be replaced by a growing demand for concrete, believable, and accurate information.

Leo Cherne

I see advertising as trying to tell somebody something, and, if I'm trying to tell someone something, I don't get out a brass band, and I don't put on a clown suit.

Fairfax M. Cone

Advertising is what you do when you can't go see somebody. That's all it is.

Fairfax M. Cone

You can tell the ideals of a nation by its advertisements.

Norman Douglas

If you remember the joke in my commercial while forgetting my product, the joke is really on my client. If my presenter grabs you but you ignore what she's trying to tell you, I've blown it. If you are struck by my cleverness but remain unsold by my ideas, I've bombed as a copywriter.

If you award my commercial a sterling-silver bowl for excellence without asking how well it worked, you've given me an empty bowl. In the pursuit of creative advertising we must be careful not to take our eye off what advertising must accomplish. The very things that are remembered most may contribute least to making the sale. They may even detract from the sale.

Alvin Hampel

Advertising is found in societies which have passed the point of satisfying the basic animal needs.

Marion Harper, Jr.

If I were asked to name the deadliest subversive force within capitalism—the single greatest source of its waning morality—I would without hesitation name advertising.

Robert L. Heilbroner

My commitment is to give the consumer what she wants; and if her wants have an emotional component to them, it behooves me to recognize that fact.

Donald M. Kendall

The amount of shoddy advertising must be a significant factor in the average consumer's concept of American business and the American businessman. Sensible people, I believe, are entitled to be somewhat skeptical of business organizations responsible for the tasteless and uninformative ads that are often stock-in-trade today. If the public's image of American business is an increasingly tarnished one, I, for one, attribute that in some measure to business' most visible product—its own advertising.

Miles W. Kirkpatrick

The product that will not sell without advertising, will not sell profitably with advertising.

Albert Lasker

You can fool all of the people all of the time if the advertising is right and the budget is big enough.

Joseph E. Levine

The man who on his trade relies
Must either bust or advertise.

Thomas Lipton

Nothing except the mint can make money without advertising.

Thomas B. Macaulay

I don't believe that advertising ever gets you a quality reputation. If you don't have it, advertising won't help you a bit. And if you do have it, word of mouth is enough.

F. James McDonald

Advertising in the final analysis should be news. If it is not news it is worthless.

Adolph S. Ochs

The new breed of advertising people have no regard for how well an ad sells the product. These pseudo-intellectuals who are now flocking to advertising, these callow, half-baked, overpaid young men and women haven't the slighest interest in how the consuming public reacts to stimuli any more than abstract painters have.

David Ogilvy

Most of the people who write advertising today have never had to sell anything to anybody. They've never seen a consumer.

David Ogilvy

Advertising is the place where the selfish interests of the manufacturer coincide with the interests of society.

David Ogilvy

It has taken more than a hundred scientists two years to find out how to make the product. . . . I have been given thirty days to create its personality and even plan its launching. If I do my job well, I shall contribute as much as the hundred scientists to the success of the product.

David Ogilvy

Advertising is not spending; it's an investment to get a piece of the mind of millions of Americans.

Alph B. Peterson

I believe that advertising is an investment where risk taking is inordinately rewarded and where the penalty for failure is not correspondingly severe.

Charles A. Posey

Critics of advertising think the consumer is an idiot. They think we think so too. On the contrary, we rely on the consumer's intelligence to listen, to compare, to be convinced by our best arguments. We rely on his or her interest in new products, new benefits, new ways of putting goods to use, to profit, and to enjoyment.

Sam Thurm

Half the money I spend on advertising is wasted, and the trouble is I don't know which half.

John Wanamaker

Advertising cannot make people buy against their wills. It cannot induce repeated purchases of inferior products. It cannot prolong the life of a product that has outlived its usefulness or which has been outmoded. The power of advertising is limited. And the thousands of net product failures are testimony to the fact that, if something does not fill a need, fulfill an aspiration, or provide some comfort or solace, real or emotional, it cannot succeed no matter how many dollars are invested in advertising.

Edward B. Wilson II

AFFLUENT SOCIETY

The price of an affluent society may be that by the time one is well enough off to turn the dirty work over to someone else there will be no one willing to do it.

W. Willard Wirtz

AGREEMENT

If two men on the same job agree all the time, then one is useless. If they disagree all the time, then both are useless.

Darryl F. Zanuck

AGRICULTURE

Our urban friends in the nonfarming part of American society seem to think that agriculture is a completely subsidized, noncompetitive industry—that every farmer has a guaranteed income—and that farmers are in effect wards of the government. Nothing could be farther from the truth. The plain fact is that there is still more competition and more risk in agriculture than in industry. There are literally hundreds of thousands of farmers all producing the same products. Show me an industry—any industry—with that kind of competition.

J. Phil Campbell

AMERICA

America is not a land of money, but of wealth—not a land of rich people, but successful workers.

Henry Ford

We Americans talk a great deal about how inventive we are, yet most of the world's great ideas did not originate on this continent. They are European or Chinese or Arabian or who knows what. What Americans have been good at is not invention but innovation—putting ideas to use. And that derives from the capitalist environment.

Benjamin A. Rogge

When most Americans read about the corruption and ruthlessness of the rich, they are inclined to grin. Their malefactors are their dream-selves. The American does not aspire to overthrow the thieves and oppressors half as much as he does to become one of them.

Ben Hecht

ANNUAL MEETING

It will come as a surprise to some of you, but annual meetings aren't the favorite task of most corporate chairmen. Indeed, some of my colleagues have assured me that the greatest benefit of retiring is never having to face another.

David Rockefeller

ANTITRUST

Very few concepts have had as little critical analysis and undergone fewer changes in the past 80 years than antitrust. All of the patches that have been added to the antitrust quilt during that period have been cut from the same bolt of cloth—a vague, semi-emotional feeling that bigness is bad or dangerous or the associated ill-formed concept that economic concentration is bad or dangerous.

James J. Ling

Antitrust is the greatest thing barristers and lawyers ever had happen to them.

Ian D. Sinclair

ART AND TECHNOLOGY

When I love you, I teach you the art. When I tolerate you I teach you the technology.

James L. Hayes

ARTIST

A man who works with his hands is a laborer; a man who works with his hands and his brain is a craftsman; but a man who works with his hands and his brain and his heart is an artist.

Louis Nizer

ASSETS

If you count all your assets you always show a profit.

Robert Quillen

AUTOMATION

Automized and computerized industry requires more and more young men and women who have white-collar skills but behave with the docility of blue-collar workers.

Staughton Lynd

AUTOMOBILE

The car has become a secular sanctuary for the individual, his mobile Walden Pond.

Edward McDonagh

B

BANKERS

Historically, the bankers have tried to portray themselves as tribal priests and the banks have been built on the model of temples.

Edward J. Kane

BANKING

Banking is a risk industry. Unless bankers take risks, they cannot support their communities nor the industries and businesses making up those communities.

Philip E. Coldwell

A sound banker is not one who foresees danger and avoids it, but one who, when he is ruined, is ruined in a conventional and orthodox way so that no one can really blame him.

John Maynard Keynes

Banking is perhaps the most personal of the big businesses.

Martin Mayer

If I owe a million dollars, then I am lost. But if I owe 50 million, then the bankers are lost.

Celso Ming

We're more than a bank. If we have to say "No" to a customer, we say, "No, because . . ."

Donald Sneed, Jr.

It is rather a pleasant experience to be alone in a bank at night.

Willie Sutton

It should not be the aim of public policy to make banking a no-risk business. The usefulness of banks to society depends in large part on their ability to evaluate risks and their willingness to accept them. This is their function. This is how they contribute to the efficient allocation of economic resources. Banking without risk-taking would be a sterile, even a parasitical, business.

Ellmore C. Patterson

BANKRUPTCY

An honest man can go bankrupt and retain his reputation, if he has clearly done the best that he can and protected his creditors to the extent of his ability.

Winthrop W. Aldrich

Bankruptcy is when you put your money in your hip pocket and let your creditors take your coat.

Bob Edwards

If you are going bankrupt, be sure you go bankrupt on a big scale.

Paul A. Samuelson

BANKS

If you owe a bank enough money you own it.

Anonymous

BELL SYSTEM

The Bell system is like a big dragon. You kick it in the tail, and two years later, it feels it in its head.

Frederick Kappel

BIG BUSINESS

Big business breeds bureaucracy and bureaucrats exactly as big government does.

T. K. Quinn

The growth of a large business is merely the survival of the fittest.

John D. Rockefeller

We are toying too much with the effect of big business instead of studying the causes.

Emil Schram

BIGNESS

If we can't do business observing certain absolute standards, we will simply demur from doing business. Instead of growing another $30 million in sales, we'll grow a little less, but we'll sleep better for it.

W. Michael Blumenthal

The dinosaur's eloquent lesson is that if some bigness is good, an overabundance of bigness is not necessarily better.

Eric Johnston

You need large companies and their large capital to progress. After all, you can't build a Lockheed-1011 in your garage.

Robert H. Volk

No company and no industry in the American economy is yet big enough to bring enough goods to enough people.

Charles E. Wilson

BOARDROOM

The road to the boardroom leads through the locker room.

David Riesman

BOLDNESS

It takes a great deal of boldness mixed with a vast deal of caution to acquire a great fortune; but then it takes 10 times as much wit to keep it after you have got it as it took you to make it.

Baron Rothschild

BONDS

Gentlemen prefer bonds.

Andrew Mellon

BOSS

Boss your boss as soon as you can; try it on early. There is nothing he will like so well if he is the right kind of boss; if he is not, he is not the man for you to remain with.

Andrew Carnegie

BOTTOM LINE

The only thing that matters is the bottom line? What a presumptuous thing to say. The bottom line is in heaven.

Edwin Land

BRAIN DRAIN

The most wasteful brain drain in America today is the drain in the kitchen sink.

Elizabeth Gould Davis

BUDGETING

Just about the time you think you can make both ends meet, somebody moves the ends.

Pansy Penner

BUREAUCRACY

In many ways, regulations are creating a subtle bureaucratization of industry. You don't take risks; you think like a bureaucrat.

Murray L. Weidenbaum

Bureaucracy defends the status quo long past the time when the quo has lost its status.

Laurence J. Peter

BUSINESS

Business is more exciting than any game.

Lord Beaverbrook

The business framework is not merely where we produce and distribute the world's goods and services; it is the terrain on which we meet, interact with each other, work out our ambitions, achieve or fail to achieve our purposes as we see them.

W. Michael Blumenthal

Business is a workhorse, a mule—and do you ask a mule to be a Pegasus?

Kenneth E. Boulding

In the field of modern business, so rich in opportunity for the exercise of man's finest and most varied mental faculties and moral qualities, mere money-making cannot be regarded as a legitimate end . . . since with the conduct of business, human happiness or misery is inextricably interwoven.

Louis D. Brandeis

There is not an appetite or need, human desire or human satisfaction which is not at the core of the energy we call business. Without need, we in business are nothing.

Leo Cherne

The business of business is America.

Leo Cherne

The business of America is business.

Calvin Coolidge

Business will be better or worse.

Calvin Coolidge

If business is to be considered a continuous process, instead of a series of disjointed stop-and-go events, then the economic universe in which a business operates—and all the major events within it—must have rhyme, rhythm, or reason.

Peter F. Drucker

Business is too important to be left to businessmen.

John Kenneth Galbraith

In today's society, business is not being measured by the specific goods produced or services rendered, but by the totality of its influence and contributions to the whole community. Hence, wild ducks, public parks, ecology, factors which may seem far afield from operating a business—are now vital parts of decisions being made at the office.

J. Edgar Hoover

Never acquire a business you don't know how to run.

Robert W. Johnson

Whenever you're sitting across from some important person, always picture him sitting there in a suit of long red underwear. That's the way I always operated in business.

Joseph P. Kennedy

Business today consists in persuading crowds.

Gerald Stanley Lee

Business is the oldest of the arts, the newest of the professions.

Laurence Lowell

Business more than any other occupation is a continual dealing with the future; it is a continual calculation, an instinctive exercise in foresight.

Henry R. Luce

Business is a combination of war and sport.

Andre Maurois

Leaving business at the office sounds like a good rule ... but a man who intends to make a success should be collecting ideas and tips and mapping out programs during every waking hour.

John H. Patterson

Business is like a man rowing a boat upstream. He has no choice; he must go ahead or he will go back.

Lewis E. Pierson

I don't know of anyone today that has less influence in this country than business.

Ronald Reagan

The choice being faced by business is not to do or not to do, but to do or have done to it.

Harold M. Williams

Business is like riding a bicycle. Either you keep moving or you fall down.

John David Wright

BUSINESS ACTIVISTS

We live today with laws written largely by dewy-eyed idealists—by people with little understanding of the economic or even the technological consequences of these laws. How much better if corporate America recognized the legitimacy of the public interest and brought our technical and economic expertise to the drafting table. What I am suggesting is a proactive, rather than a reactive role—as partners, not adversaries. To do this, we must have an ability to anticipate social interests and validly to participate in the search for solutions to social problems.... We must raise our sights beyond the comfortable limits of our day-to-day operations. We must become society watchers and students of the nonbusiness world around us; further we must master ways of influencing our social environment.

Donald C. Carroll

BUSINESS AND GOVERNMENT

In the years immediately ahead, we are going to have to develop a workable system of cooperative government-business enterprise going far beyond anything we've achieved up to this point. Business is now being asked to solve, or to join with government in solving, a whole series of social and other ills, that are shaking the foundations of our society. But some way must be found, in turning business' attention to these pressing needs, to preserve the profit motive—the essential ingredient of private enterprise. Unless business is to be allowed to seek *business* solutions, these public needs will not be met; because there simply will not be enough taxpayers' dollars available for government alone to finance the solutions.

John T. Connor

This is business country... and it wants a business government. I do not mean a government by business, nor a government for business, but I do mean a government that will understand business.

Calvin Coolidge

What is needed is recognition of the fact that, between government, business, and the public, there is a triangular community of interest. Clearly, it is in business' interest to shape its behavior to prevailing public values; it is more efficient to do so than not to do so. It is also clear that government is the high-cost alternative through which public values are imposed on corporations that do not accurately perceive these values.

Juanita M. Kreps

The fact seems to be that business, particularly retailers, has hardly been talking to government. When it has talked, it has been primarily as an antagonist. We've got to work with government.

Charles Y. Lazarus

We should not have and do not have any quarrel with the concept of government as an umpire. It is a wholly appropriate role that we can and do accept. But in an era where government seems increasingly to assume an adversary role in the nation's industry, then government is no longer the umpire. It becomes the other team. This we should not and cannot and will not accept. Much too much is at stake.

Warren W. Lebeck

I want to proclaim a new doctrine: a complete separation of business and government.

J. P. Morgan

While I believe very strongly that there has to be an element of free enterprise in our business, and in the freedom of executive decision in day-to-day affairs, I also believe that government involvement can lead to more efficiency. Generally, stockholders are poorly informed and generally they ask for information only when things go wrong. Sometimes that is too late. Governments make you constantly accountable.

Alex Park

The best minds are not in government. If any were, business would hire them away.

Ronald Reagan

We find ourselves in an adversary relationship with the bureaucracy. We must find a way of making government a partner with business.

Irving S. Shapiro

Business is probably one of the least organized and least aggressive sectors of society in terms of explaining its needs and positions to the government.

Arthur R. Taylor

BUSINESS AND SOCIETY

We expect our business activities to make social sense and our social activities to make business sense.

Business Roundtable

Business activity is necessarily a private activity which, for its own good and its own justification, has to strive for the common good and the stated ends of society. Business enterprise is thus seen as local, autonomous self government which, by serving the ends of society, serves its own self-interests and guarantees its own survival.

Peter Drucker

BUSINESS BLUNDERS

Many blunder in business through inability or an unwillingness to adopt new ideas. I have seen many a success turn to failure also, because the thought which should be trained on big things is cluttered up with the burdensome detail of little things.

Philip S. Delaney

BUSINESS CREDIBILITY

To me, this concern about business credibility is only a part of a much wider concern I have about general morality today. It occurs at all levels ... a lack of concern for other people, an attempt to get away with all that you think you can get away with. I see this in every facet of society.

Walter A. Haas

BUSINESS CRITICISM

Those critics [of business] whose aim is destructive are following a basic tactic of divisiveness—and with considerable success. They are endeavoring to turn various segments of our society against business. They are trying to make America a society at war with itself. Their ultimate aim is to alienate the American consumer from business, to tear down long-established relationships which have served both so well.

James M. Roche

American business is so widely owned and its benefits so widely dispersed that when we criticize business, we are in effect, criticizing ourselves. When business does not do the job expected of it, it is we—all of us—who are both accountable and concerned.

James M. Roche

BUSINESS DEALS

I am first and foremost a catalyst. I bring people and situations together. That's the big thing—bringing the deal together.

Armand Hammer

BUSINESS EDUCATION

Business education is a complete waste of time, because it just cannot be taught. It is not an exact science, and so you have to use common sense to succeed in it.

William Black

The top business schools do a good job. If the schools could concentrate on a little instruction in humility it would be helpful. You just don't come fresh out of business school ready to run a large corporation.

Reginald H. Jones

BUSINESS ENTERPRISE

Look back along the endless corridors of time and you will see that four things have built civilization: the spirit of religion; the spirit of creative art; the spirit of research and the spirit of business enterprise.

Neil Carothers

BUSINESS ESTABLISHMENT

The advocates of consumerism, unionism, government intervention are exciting. We are the establishment. We are often dull.

Louis T. Hagopian

BUSINESS FUNCTIONS

Business has only two functions—marketing and innovation.

Peter F. Drucker

BUSINESS IMAGE

Business today is so unpopular in this country that it may become dangerous even for the Secretary of Commerce to venture a word in its defense.

Peter G. Peterson

The philosopher Alfred North Whitehead is remembered for saying that in a great society businessmen think greatly of their function. Today, that comment ought to be turned the other way. A society which thinks poorly of its businessmen and deeply distrusts their motives is not a great society but a society in trouble. We are in danger of demolishing our own house and hanging the carpenter.

Irving S. Shapiro

BUSINESS-JAPAN

My concept is that a company is a fate-sharing body. So to make a good business we have to work together.

Akio Morita

BUSINESS LEADERSHIP

Not so long ago, the stereotypic business executive was a hard-driving supersalesman, an efficiency expert, a bottom-liner, a bit of a pirate, the man who actually thought that what was good for his company was good for his country. Such people are going the way of the dinosaur; they are simply not equipped for business leadership today. Society has imposed, and will continue to impose, constraints [which] demand a much different kind of business leadership today. Leaders now must be valid participants in the formulation of public policy or else be victims of it. A contemporary leader must genuinely understand the public interest, as well as his her personal economic interest.

Donald C. Carroll

The most outstanding business firms of the future will be those whose leadership is skilled in the interface problems—technology with economics, marketing with social change, and business with government. The time has passed when good business management can narrowly focus merely on design, manufacture, and attempts to sell products oblivious to the broader society. Such management will satisfy neither the individuals working in their companies nor the individual buyers in the marketplace.

Simon Ramo

BUSINESSPEOPLE

It somehow amazes me that the American businessman, who has at his disposal all the resources, techniques and knowledge for selling his product, still hasn't done a good job selling himself to the younger generation.

Werner A. Baum

I believe that the able industrial leader who creates wealth and employment is more worthy of historical notice than politicians or soldiers.

J. Paul Getty

My father always told me that all businessmen were sons of bitches, but I never believed it until now.

John F. Kennedy

Every successful enterprise requires three men—a dreamer, a businessman, and a son-of-a-bitch.

Peter McArthur

A businessman is a hybrid of a dancer and a calculator.

Paul Valery

BUSY-NESS

If your business keeps you so busy that you have no time for anything else, there must be something wrong, either with you or with your business.

William J. H. Boetcker

C

CANDOR

One of the most conspicuous trends in our society is the desire and demand for openness, particularly by the young. The demand for candor is, on the whole, a good, if occasionally a painful, thing for a company. Candor forces the company to define its problems more precisely since it can't hide behind a lot of self-defensive euphemisms. Having defined its problems, the company is more likely to attack them rationally and solve them. I feel this kind of corporate honesty will pay off, both for the individual company, and for business as a whole.

Peter G. Peterson

CAPITAL

The highest use of capital is not to make money, but make money do more for the betterment of life.

Henry Ford

Capital is what makes capitalism work.

James J. Needham

CAPITAL AND LABOR

Big business can't prosper without small business to supply its needs and buy its products. Labor can't prosper so long as capital lies idle. Capital can't prosper while labor is unemployed.

DeWitt M. Emery

CAPITALISM

The dynamics of capitalism is postponement of enjoyment to the constantly postponed future.

Norman O. Brown

The trouble with socialism is socialism. The trouble with capitalism is capitalists.

William F. Buckley

Capitalism is the only system in the world founded on credit and character.

Hubert Eaton

I'd say capitalism's worst excess is in the large number of crooks and tinhorns who get too much of the action.

Malcolm Forbes

I sometimes suspect that many American capitalists actually distrust the market as much as capitalism's enemies do.... There are whole industries today that prefer to escape the market's discipline.

Henry Ford II

There is no more demoralizing theory than that which imputes all human evils to capitalism or any other single agency.

Samuel Gompers

We are too mealy mouthed. We fear the word capitalism is unpopular. So we talk about the free enterprise system and run to cover in the folds of the flag and talk about the American Way of Life.

Eric A. Johnston

American capitalism has been both overpraised and overindicted . . . it is neither the Plumed Knight nor the monstrous robber baron.

Max Lerner

Capitalism cannot be expected to function efficiently except on its own terms in a social atmosphere that allows sufficient freedom of action.

Joseph A. Schumpeter

The whole point of free enterprise—of capitalism—is vigorous, honest competition. Every corner cut, every bribe placed, every little cheating move by a businessman in pursuit of quick plunder instead of honest profit is an outright attack on the real free enterprise system.

William E. Simon

CAREER

I cannot honestly claim that I possessed any innate talent nor even a particular desire for a business career.

J. Paul Getty

CATALYST

I am first and foremost a catalyst. I bring people and situations together.

Armand Hammer

CEO

The typical successful executives are overwhelmingly interested in their work. They don't play very much. If they get out on the golf course, it's to win. They don't dally. They aren't widely read either. What they do have is a tremendous drive—so they aren't heavy drinkers. They are not heavy anything except heavy workers. They have a desire to prove to themselves that they really can overcome impossible obstacles.

Chester Burger

A chief executive officer has to discover what is effective—how he can make people listen, how he can be persuasive, how he can lead and motivate. If a CEO can't, then he's not very good—he'll be eaten up by the troops.

A. W. Clausen

Every CEO I've ever talked to, once pushed into a corner with two martinis, will tell you that though the myth is that he stands with the reins of power in his hands, his big question is not "How shall I drive this marvelous chariot?" but "How the hell can I get these goddam horses to move their asses at all?"

Geoffrey C. Hazard

A chief executive has lots of power and authority. It's a heady experience. If he's not careful he grows to believe that he's the only one who can make decisions. He may bottleneck his company.

Arthur F. Kelly

I don't think anyone over 70 should be a chief executive of a large corporation. Corporations recognize that the pressures on a chief execu-tive have increased dramatically. Executives burn out more, so it's appropriate to lower the mandatory retirement age for the boss. It also helps the morale of a corporation to have turnover at the top. There are a lot of young bucks waiting to be the chief.

Arjay Miller

The chief executive's ability to influence the corporation is by no means absolute. Fifty years ago, many chief executives were very dominant figures who could do just about anything. That really has changed. No chief executive today can very long take measures that go contrary to strong views within the organization. He might get away with it for a bit, but sooner or later it would catch up with him, and he would find himself out of a job.

David Rockefeller

CHAIRMAN OF THE BOARD

The chairman should be the one to put pressure on the management team for the sake of the board members. He has to be far enough away to see things more as an outsider. The chairman is responsible for making sure that the board and the management can take time occasionally to analyze what they are doing and where they are going. Maybe even consider whether they're even in the right business.

Robert Lynch

CHANGE

It is easy to mislead ourselves into thinking there is something preordained about our profit-motivated, free-market, private-enterprise system that is, as they say of gold, universal and immutable. I personally believe it is the system which offers the human individual the greatest hope in the world. But its status in that world is not guaranteed. It must be earned. And it can be earned and enhanced only if it recognizes and uses its own greatest strengths: its innate adaptability and its capacity to manage change to provide services which society as a whole desires or needs—and cannot achieve as well through other means.

A. W. Clausen

Some folks are continually making changes. I flatter myself that I like new ventures and new experiences. But when it comes to fundamentals, I'm a poor changer. I believe it's best to find the right foundations and build on them.

William H. Danforth

People may change their minds as often as their coats, and new sets of rules of conduct may be written every week, but the fact remains that human nature has not changed and does not change, that inherent human beliefs stay the same, the fundamental rules of human conduct continue to hold.

Lammot du Pont

Industries and businesses that must operate in the marketplace of free choice know that they must change, they must adapt, they must accommodate to changes in public attitudes—or they will surely die.

William D. Ruckelshaus

The only thing that we can predict with certainty is change.

Jayne Spain

CHARACTER

The first thing is character. . . . Because a man I do not trust could not get money from me on all the bonds in Christendom.

J. P. Morgan

CHARITY

Charity is injurious unless it helps the recipient to become independent of it.

John D. Rockefeller, Jr.

CHERISHING

As you cherish the things most worthwhile in your family life, cherish the things most worthwhile in your company.

Wm. B. Given, Jr.

CHIEF EXECUTIVE

I don't believe in just ordering people to do things. You have to sort of grab an oar and row with them. My philosophy is to stay as close as possible to what's happening. If I can't solve something, how the hell can I expect my managers to?

Harold S. Geneen

If you're the chief executive you get more blame than you deserve and you also get more credit than you deserve. If you want one, you've got to accept the other too.

K. T. Keller

Not all chief executives are temperamentally capable of accepting and assimilating information which happens to conflict with their own personal values and predilections.

Robert N. McMurry

CHISELING

If we are chiselers, we are chiselers for our stockholders. I want a dollar for a dollar—or, better yet, $1.10.

Charles G. Bluhdorn

COMMITTEE

A committee is a cul de sac down which ideas are lured and then quietly strangled.

Barnett Cocks

COMMUNICATION

Electronic engineers have yet to devise a better interoffice communication system than the water cooler.

Leo Ellis

The businessman only wants two things said about his company—what he pays his public relations people to say and what he pays his advertising people to say. He doesn't like anybody ever to look above, beyond, or over that.

Don S. Hewitt

One problem facing businessmen is lack of articulateness. They may be good at this or that, but they are still regarded as inarticulate. For myself I delight in throwing out information about our company. That is part of my job: to project knowledge about our company into the minds of people—what the company is doing, why, and what it hopes to do. If that's garrulous, then I'm garrulous. I will talk to anyone who will listen.

Ian MacGregor

A hallmark of American business is its willingness to keep up with the times—to innovate. Yet, before the press, radio, or television, the businessman comes on like the original Neanderthal man, mouthing cliches that went out with the Stone Age.

Donald S. McNaughton

COMPETENCE

It isn't the incompetent who destroy an organization. The incompetent never get in a position to destroy it. It is those who have achieved something and want to rest upon their achievements who are forever clogging things up.

Charles Sorenson

COMPETITION

The first man gets the oyster; the second man gets the shell.

Andrew Carnegie

Businessmen love free enterprise but hate competition.

Lewis A. Engman

We find the instinct to shut out competition deep-rooted even among banks and corporations, among corner grocers and haberdasheries, among peanut vendors and shoeshine boys.

James A. Farley

We've long believed there's nothing to be gained by telling our competitors how we do things.

Edward G. Harness

Hard-nosed competition is the best assurance of a healthy business. It has done more to modernize our plants, more to train our people, improve our systems, and broaden our product line than any other force on earth, including pride, ambition, and naked greed.

Donald M. Kendall

When it comes to competition—well, if they are drowning I'd put a hose in their mouth. I've a feeling about competitors that I've tried to get across in McDonald's. Competitors are somebody you learn to hate. There is no nice way of being in business and loving your competitors.

Ray Kroc

It is ridiculous to call this an industry. This is rat eat rat, dog eat dog. I'll kill 'em, and I'm going to kill 'em before they kill me. You're talking about the American way of survival of the fittest.

Ray Kroc

Anyone who has been in sports cannot help feeling the thrill of competitiveness. In business, there is a carryover. You should at least respond to competition. When you get an order that your competitor might have received, you should enjoy a feeling of accomplishment. Our competitive free-enterprise system is built on this spirit, and that is the spirit that is being so abused today. Some claim we are losing it. Some claim we have lost it.

William S. Lowe

Competition is like horse manure. It's everywhere.

R. Wayne Oldham

I don't meet competition, I crush it.

Charles Revson

The trouble in American life today, in business as well as in sports, is that too many people are afraid of competition.

Knute Rockne

Competition brings out the best in products and the worst in people.

David Sarnoff

The idea of imposing restrictions on a free economy to assure freedom of competition is like breaking a man's leg to make him run faster.

Morris R. Sayre

Whenever I may be tempted to slack up and let the business run for awhile on its own impetus, I picture my competitor sitting at a desk in his opposition house, thinking and thinking with the most devilish intensity and clearness, and I ask myself what I can do to be prepared for his next brilliant move.

H. Gordon Selfridge

The ferociousness of competition among business enterprises is a locomotive of innovational development and enrichment. The modern market economy, with its freedom of private initiative and the bracing energy of competition, is a powerful tool for material progress.

Jean-Jacques Servan-Schreiber

There is no resting place for an enterprise in a competitive economy.

Alfred P. Sloan

COMPLIANCE

[Business] will only retain its present relative freedom by voluntarily aligning its internal policies with clearly expressed national goals. If business everywhere will pursue the spirit as well as the letter of equal opportunity, there is apt to be less retraining legislation and, in the long run, greater respect for business. Business will retain its freedom of action by voluntarily doing always more than the law requires, voluntarily doing always less than the law permits.

J. Irwin Miller

COMPUTERS

The main impact of the computer has been the provision of unlimited jobs for clerks.

Peter Drucker

CONCENTRATION

My motto is first honesty, then industry, then concentration.

Andrew Carnegie

Put all eggs in one basket and then watch that basket.

Andrew Carnegie

Concentration, far from being unwholesome, may be desirable, even indispensable, if it means that through a concentration of money, skills, and management, a job is done that otherwise would not be done.

Crawford H. Greenewalt

Concentration in an industry, in and of itself, does not constitute a violation of antitrust laws or a basis for divestiture.

Ross L. Makone

CONFIDENCE

Confidence is the foundation of all business relations. The degree of confidence a man has in others, and the degree of confidence others have in him, determines a man's standing in the commercial and industrial world.

William J. H. Boetcker

CONGLOMERATES

The real key to conglomerate success is the internal growth which only acquisitions make possible.

George T. Scharffenberger

I hate conglomerates. Excellence and size are fundamentally incompatible.

Robert C. Townsend

CONGLOMERATEURS

Today's Horatio Alger capitalists just go out and get a contract from the military-industrial complex. They're virtually faceless partisans of state capitalism. Even the conglomerateurs are awful tame compared with such flamboyant characters as Jay Gould and J. P. Morgan.

Matthew Josephson

CONSCIENCE

A business must have a conscience as well as a counting house.

Montague Burton

I never met a corporation yet that had a conscience.

George Meany

CONSULTANTS

Consultants are people who borrow your watch, tell you what time it is, and then walk off with the watch.

Robert Townsend

CONSUMERS

Consumers with dollars in their pockets are not, by any stretch of their imagination, weak. To the contrary, they are the most merciless, meanest, toughest market disciplinarians I know.

Max E. Brunk

The consumer is eventually in control of the markets, so there is no question that business must satisfy the consumer.

William K. Eastham

The consumer game is tougher than pro football and more conniving than chess. One side [industry] invents the rules and the other side [consumers] is left to guess what they are.

Betty Furness

If American industry continues to sow contempt for the consumer, it will reap contempt from the consumer.

Betty Furness

My commitment is to give the consumer what she wants; and if her wants have an emotional component to them, it behooves me to recognize that fact.

Donald M. Kendall

Much of the public's antipathy toward big business is rooted in the American consumer's own bad experiences in the marketplace. To the extent that it is rooted there, it can be remedied only there. We counter the threat of government over-regulation when we satisfy our customers, when we do business as business should be done, openly and honestly, with the customer's needs uppermost in mind.

Thomas A. Murphy

The consumer is not a moron. She is your wife.

David Ogilvy

CONSUMER CONFIDENCE

Consumer confidence in an industry can be a very fragile thing. It only takes a few builders who promise but don't deliver, who cheat rather than perform, who delay until the warranty expires rather than repair, to damage the reputation of an entire industry.

Virginia H. Knauer

CONSUMER INFORMATION

Consumer ignorance acts as a subsidy to inefficient plants.

Sumner H. Slichten

CONSUMERISM

The consumer movement is at a critical point in its history, and we face a critical danger—the danger that we will be fooled by fake reform. Deceptive packaging and mislabeling are as insidious on the congressional calendar as they are on the supermarket shelf.

Bess Myerson Grant

The essence of the consumer movement is not that business will be saddled with burdensome restrictions, reporting requirements, and regulations. It is, rather, new and altered relationships in the marketplace; new factors to be considered in design, production, and distribution; and new responsibility for social consequences hitherto taken for granted.

Warren G. Magnuson

The word consumerism has come to connote dissatisfaction, complaint, and fraudulent business practices. Consumerism should have a more positive meaning—it should stand for satisfying the customer. In this very real sense, consumerism is what our free-enterprise system is all about. There is only one way a business can earn a profit, and that is to make a product a consumer wants to buy, produce it efficiently, provide good service, and treat the consumer honestly and fairly.

James M. Roche

When business sees consumerism and its spokesmen as enemies of the system, then business is demonstrating its own failure to understand the healthy tensions and competing pressures that must be always present in that system, if it is to survive.

Edward B. Rust

Members of the "disaster lobby" look back with fond nostalgia to the "good old days" when there weren't any nasty factories to pollute the air and kill the animals and drive people to distraction with misleading advertisements. But what was life really like in America 150 years ago?

Whatever American businessmen have done to bring us out of that paradise of 150 years ago, I say let's give them a grateful pat on the back—not a knife in it.

Thomas R. Shepard Jr.

Consumerism is getting more and more business leaders out of their executive suites and into the marketplace they should have visited before. They are discovering sources of consumer dissatisfaction they never knew existed. They are improving communications and customer relations, checking on services and advertising warranties, finding out what makes customers buy—and becoming better chief executives as a result.

Theodore C. Sorensen

It is a false assumption that the consumer has the unquestioned, unqualified right to instant perfection in the marketplace.

Woodrow Wirsig

CONSUMER PRODUCTS

In the days ahead, the management of any consumer goods company is going to have only two options: built a trouble-free product, or be ready to fix the product fast.

S. E. Knudsen

In a consumer society, the best product you can manufacture is the one that must be replaced immediately.

Gene Lees

CONSUMER RELATIONS

The responsiveness of a firm to the consumer is directly proportionate to the distance on the organization chart from the consumer to the chairman of the board.

Virginia K. Knauer

CONSUMER SAFETY

The safety of the consumer is an imperative. There can be no justification—economic or moral—to take chances that an informed consumer would not take. The consuming public has responsibilities as well. It has an obligation to be informed, to maintain its sense of proportion. The consuming public should recognize that industry is a part of society, and not separate. It should appreciate that we are trying with all our strength to be responsive, and that we are not driven by economic motivations alone, but that if sometimes this appears to be the case, it is because ours is the difficult role of converting ideas and wishes into practical applications. The public might even have a little empathy for the position we are in—trying to reconcile a contradictory array of public priorities and objectives in order to guide our actions.

Howard C. Harder

CONSUMER SOCIETY

In a consumer society there are inevitably two kinds of slaves: the prisoners of addiction and the prisoners of envy.

Ivan Illich

CONTRADICTION

I have heard speakers . . . use the phrase, "I can say without fear of contradiction . . . ." Anyone who uses this in a modern democracy or to the shareholders of a modern company, should see a doctor.

Lord Chandos

CONTROL

I will not go on the board of a company that I don't control.

Thomas A. Edison

CONTROLS

Wage and price controls are military solutions to economic problems.

Irving Kristol

CORNERSTONES

The four cornerstones on which the structure of this nation was built are: Initiative, Imagination, Individuality, and Independence.

Edward V. Rickenbacker

CORPORATE CITIZENSHIP

We've always felt we had an obligation to not only bring home the bacon to our stockholders, and to do that aggressively as well, but also to be a good national citizen.

William Kieschnick

CORPORATE IMAGE

The concept of corporate image was innocent enough in the beginning. But then we began to perceive that an image could be shaped independent of reality. Business began to concern itself not with how to present itself to the public most accurately, but whether to maintain a high profile or a low profile, about the impact of alternative synthetic images than with the authenticity of our image. And so we in business find ourselves bracketed with politicians who make decisions in secret, who shade the truth, who view public opinion as something to be managed and manipulated.

Preston Robert Tisch

CORPORATE POWER

A preoccupation with the so-called bottom line coupled with a lust for expansion is creating an environment in which few businessmen honor the traditional values; where responsibility is increasingly disassociated from the exercise of power; where skill in financial manipulations is valued more than actual knowledge and experience; where attention and effort are directed mostly to short-term considerations, regardless of long-term consequences. Political and economic power are increasingly being concentrated among a few large corporations and their officers—power they can apply against society, government, and individuals. Through their control of vast resources, these large corporations have become, in effect, another branch of government. They often exercise the power of government, but without the checks and balances inherent in our democratic system.

Hyman G. Rickover

CORPORATE RESPONSIBILITY

A healthy and stable society is the best kind of society in which to do business. And the company which adds to that health and stability is doing itself a favor.

W. F. Rockwell, Jr.

CORPORATE TAXES

Corporations don't pay taxes. People do. Businesses are people. To punish businesses through higher taxes will mean higher unemployment, higher prices for consumers, lower real earnings for workers.

William E. Simon

CORPORATION

U.S. Steel is the prototype of the corporation of the first third of this century, General Motors of the second third of the century, and IBM of the last third of the century.

Daniel Bell

At some point in the life cycle of virtually every corporation, its ability to succeed in spite of itself runs out.

Richard Brien

The head of a corporation has two constituencies. His primary one is the public, upon whom the corporation is dependent for its existence. His second constituency is made up of the stockholders, who place him in office, and the employees, without whom the corporation could not function. It is, therefore, not only correct that the corporation lend its good offices and full support to social involvement for the good of the public; it also happens to be one of the institutions best able to do so, for three simple reasons: Corporations have talented people who are well qualified to make contributions that go beyond immediate, day-to-day business affairs; secondly, they are structured and organized in a way which permits effective utilization of their talents; and thirdly, corporations have the means and influence with which to make significant contributions and to inspire others to do likewise.

Joseph F. Cullman III

Every large corporation should be thought of as a social enterprise; that is, an entity whose existence and decisions can be justified only insofar as they serve public or social purposes.

Robert A. Dahl

The modern corporation is a political institution: its purpose is the creation of legitimate power in the industrial sphere.

Peter Drucker

There's no doubt in my mind that the effectiveness—both economic and social—of corporations will be directly related to how much freedom of decision they allow their own people at the point which most intimately feels the impact of their decisions.

C. Peter McColough

There's been a lot of debate recently about economic dangers that result when large companies acquire other companies in unrelated industries. To me, however, the real danger—and the danger in any corporation whose top management is remote and must impose consistent business practices on the local resources it controls—is not economic. It's the danger of becoming faceless and compassionless—of being too removed to act and too isolated to understand.

C. Peter McColough

CORPORATIONS AND TECHNOLOGY

Corporations are bound to technology. Most have been created by technological breakthroughs and will change as technology changes.

Henry Wendt

CORRUPTION

It is good businessmen who are corrupting our bad politicians.

Joseph W. Falk

When I want to buy up politicians I always find the anti-monopolists the most purchaseable. They don't come so high.

William H. Vanderbilt

COSMETICS INDUSTRY

The cosmetics industry is the nastiest business in the world.

Elizabeth Arden

COSTS

There is no such thing as profit. There are only costs. Costs of doing business and costs of staying in business, costs of labor and raw materials, costs of capital, as well as the costs of today's jobs, and costs of tomorrow's jobs and tomorrow's pensions.

Peter Drucker

COUNTERFEIT

Men make counterfeit money; in many more cases, money makes counterfeit men.

Sydney J. Harris

CREATIVITY

When you try to formalize or socialize creative activity, the only sure result is commercial constipation. . . . The good ideas are all hammered out by individuals, not spewed out by groups.

Charles Brower

Somewhere along the line, there's something more. Our job is to find it and get the public accustomed to it.

Henry Ford

CREDIBILITY

In corporate reality, the bottom line is credibility. It's what sustains you when earnings go sour. It's what brings things into perspective when times are good. It is the psychological value that shapes the corporate culture, creates the unity every chief executive strives to achieve.

T. Mitchell Ford

Credibility is the number one ingredient in successfully running a major corporation. Any chief executive officer has a whole series of constituency groups—employees, stockholders, community, press, fellow businessmen. With each of these groups, you have to have a credibility that means that your views will be given serious consideration. There is no way you can lead a large organization unless your people have independently come to a judgment that you're trustworthy, have a good sense of values, and don't hand them a lot of baloney.

Irving S. Shapiro

CREDIT

Credit . . . is the only enduring testimonial to man's confidence is man.

James Blish

Owing money has never concerned me so long as I know where it could be repaid.

Henry Crown

CRISIS

When you're in a crisis, there is no time to run a study. You've got to put down on a piece of paper the 10 things that you absolutely have to do. That's what you concentrate on. Everything else—forget it.

Lee Iacocca

CRITICISM

It's sad but true that the further up you get in an organization, the less likely it is that people will tell you what you ought to hear. A lot of people are what I call "wet finger people." They hold up a wet finger to see which way the breeze is blowing. They try to guess what you have in mind. They try to anticipate your view, then give you your own view. If that's the way matters are to be decided, you don't have to have a meeting of your executives. You just scribble out orders and issue them to the troops.

Donald C. Cook

In the face of criticism, businessmen too often are silent, defensive, segmented, and far too inaccessible to journalists.

Julian Goodman

CURIOSITY

Only through curiosity can we discover opportunities and only by gambling can we take advantage of them.

Clarence Birdseye

CUSTOMER

It's the customer, and the customer alone, who casts the vote that determines how big any company should be. . . . The regulations laid down by the consuming public are far more potent and far less flexible than any code of law, merely through the exercise of the natural forces of trade.

Crawford H. Greenewalt

One of the first declarations of business philosophy I heard from my father soon after I came to work at Neiman-Marcus in 1926, was "There is never a good sale for Neiman-Marcus unless it is a good buy for the customer."

Stanley Marcus

The customer is always right.

H. Gordon Selfridge

CUSTOMER RELATIONS

Be everywhere, do everything, and never fail to astonish the customer.

Margaret Getchell

D

DEBT

A nation is not in danger of financial disaster merely because it owes itself money.

Andrew Mellon

Our dramatic trend toward a debt-based industrial complex rather than the equity based industry of 25 years ago strikes me as our most critical corporate problem. As we lean to debt, we lose the flexibility and innovative growth critical both to capitalism and to our democratic society.

Roderick M. Hills

DECISION

A decision is the action an executive must take when he has information so incomplete that the answer does not suggest itself.

Arthur W. Bradford

Whenever you see a successful business, someone once made a courageous decision.

Peter F. Drucker

DECISIONMAKING

Decisionmaking is one of the most important components for an executive. You have to say either yes or no, even though a yes or no may be wrong at the time. You can't leave people in a vacuum. Be definitive, that's important.

Helen Mayer

The business executive is by profession a decisionmaker. Uncertainty is his opponent. Overcoming it is his mission. Whether the outcome is a consequence of luck or of wisdom, the moment of decision is without doubt the most creative and critical event in the life of the executive.

John McDonald

If a man weighs over a decision, they say, "He's weighing the options." If a woman does it, they say, "She can't make up her mind."

Barbara Proctor

The task of management is not to apply a formula but to decide issues on a case-by-case basis. No fixed, inflexible rule can ever be substituted for the exercise of sound business judgment in the decision-making process.

Alfred P. Sloan, Jr.

DEFENSE INDUSTRY

We are living under the effects of what I sincerely believe is a widely held misconception: that the defense industry is a "kept" industry, eating at the public trough, that there is something basically un-American about profits on government business.

William M. Allen

DELEGATION

No matter how much work a man can do, no matter how engaging his personality may be, he will not advance far in business if he cannot work through others.

John Craig

Delegating work works, provided the one delegating works too.

Robert Half

You can delegate authority, but you can never delegate responsibility. If you picked the wrong man, the responsibility is yours—not his.

Richard E. Krafve

The best executive is one who has sense enough to pick a good man to do what he wants him to do and restraint enough to keep from meddling with him while he does it.

Paul L. Parker

The sign of a great executive is a man who can find somebody to do his job better than he can.

Jules C. Stein

None of us is irreplaceable. I have always tried to delegate responsibility. That's how you build an organization.

Lew Wasserman

DEMOCRACY

Democracy is more fun for the subordinates than it is for the superior.

Donald S. MacNaughton

DEPRESSION

Let the slump liquidate itself. Liquidate labor, liquidate stocks, liquidate the farmers, liquidate real estate. . . . It will scourge the rottenness out of the system. High costs of living will come down. People will work harder, live a more moral life. Values will be adjusted, and enterprising people will pick up the wrecks from less competent people.

Andrew Mellon

DETAILS

An executive cannot gradually dismiss details. Business is made up of details and I notice that the chief executive who dismisses them is quite likely to dismiss his business.

Success is the sum of details. It might perhaps be pleasing to imagine oneself beyond detail and engaged only in great things, but as I have often observed, if one attends only to great things and lets the little things pass, the great things become little; that is, the business shrinks.

It is not possible for an executive to hold himself aloof from anything. No business, no matter what its size, can be called safe until it has been forced to learn economy and rigidly to measure values of men and materials.

Harvey S. Firestone

DETERMINATION

According to the theory of aerodynamics, the bumblebee, because of its size, weight, and shape in relation to the total wingspread, should be unable to fly. But the bumblebee, being ignorant of these scientific truths, goes ahead and flies anyway.

Sign in a GM plant

DISASTERS

We diminish the probability of small inconveniences at the cost of increasing the probability of very large disasters.

Kenneth E. Boulding

DIVIDENDS

Do you know the only thing that gives me pleasure? It's to see my dividends coming in.

John D. Rockefeller

DOING

A man never knows what he can do until he tries to undo what he has done.

Frances Rudman

DOING ONE'S BEST

Much of the good work of the world has been that of dull people who have done their best.

George F. Hoar

DREAMS

Dreams never hurt anybody if he keeps working right behind the dream to make as much of it come real as he can.

Frank W. Woolworth

E

ECONOMIC FUTURE

If one could divine the nature of the economic forces in the world, one could foretell the future.

Robert Heilbroner

ECONOMIC GROWTH

We will not see any really substantial and intelligently directed commitment of private resources to public problems until we have developed an analytical framework by which such a commitment can be justified and monitored. We need a system where net output is increased or decreased by the amount that total assets—capital, knowledge, skills, physical and socio-political environment—are augmented or reduced as a consequence of our activities.

A. W. Clausen

ECONOMIC INDEPENDENCE

Economic independence doesn't set anyone free . . . for the higher up you go, the more responsibilities become yours.

Bernard F. Gimbel

ECONOMIC POLICY

The U.S. really does not have a national economic policy. And until we have a rational policy, businessmen can't cope with some of the conditions they face. Because of the incredible number of demands placed on business, businessmen often feel like Custer against all those Indians.

Richard P. Simmons

ECONOMIC RESEARCH

Why should industry attempt understanding and mastery through research and engineering in the field of science and technology, and yet make no similar effort in the field of economics? I can think of no aggregate of contribution that research in the physical sciences might have made during the last decade to equal that which an understanding and control of economic phenomena would have made.

Morris E. Leeds

ECONOMICS

There are only two areas where new ideas are terribly dangerous—economics and sex.

Felix Rohatyn

Most of the modern economics as taught is a form of brain damage.

E. F. Schumacher

Whenever there are great strains or changes in the economic system, it tends to generate crackpot theories which then find their way into the legislative channels.

David Stockman

ECONOMIST

An economist is a man who makes the obvious incomprehensible.

Alfred A. Knopf

ECONOMISTS

If economists were any good at business, they would be rich men instead of advisers to rich men.

Kirk Kerkorian

ECONOMY

Economy is the cutting down of other people's wages.

John B. Norton

EDUCATION

Had [executives] gone into active work during the years spent at college they would have been better educated men in every true sense of that term. The fire and energy have been stamped out of them and how to so manage as to live a life of idleness and not a life of usefulness has become the chief question with them.

Andrew Carnegie

EFFICIENCY

The efficiency of most workers is beyond the control of the management and depends more than has been supposed upon the willingness of men to do their best.

Sumner H. Slichter

Efficiency is the by-product of comfort. The enterprise that manufactures no sore backs, shoulders, wrists or behinds is at a competitive advantage over one with suffering workers.

Erwin R. Tichauer

EFFORT

There's no ceiling on effort.

Harvey C. Fruehauf

EMPLOYEES

We are a nation of employees.

George Spatts

EMPLOYERS

The employer generally gets the employees he deserves.

Sir Walter Gilbey

EMPLOYMENT

A corporation prefers to offer a job to a man who already has one, or doesn't immediately need one. The company accepts you if you are already accepted. To obtain entry into paradise, in terms of employment, you should be in a full state of grace.

Alan Harrington

Aim for employment and you head for disaster. Aim at prosperity and employment will be a by-product.

C. Northcote Parkinson

ENTERPRISE

Moralizing will not produce solutions to problems. It will not eliminate poverty; nor cure urban congestion; nor clean up rivers; nor control contaminants in the air. Only enterprise—hard-headed and creative—can accomplish these things. Enterprise flourishes in an atmosphere of personal and economic freedom.

Roy D. Chapin

ENTREPRENEURS

Going into business for yourself, becoming an entrepreneur, is the modern-day equivalent of pioneering on the old frontier.

Paula Nelson

There are few entrepreneurs who survive today. If any do, it's unusual if they don't sell out to a giant.

Jeno F. Paulucci

ENVIRONMENTALISM

The EPA has rules that would practically shut down the economy if they were put into effect.

David Stockman

ENVY

Envy is capable of serving the valuable social function of making the rich moderate their habits for fear of arousing it. It is because of the existence of envy that one does not drive Rolls Royces through the slums of Naples.

Keith Joseph

EQUITY

An exposure to equities is like the taste of blood to a young lion.

Miles Colean

A cult of equity has arisen. Buy because there's not enough to go around—the most dangerous and capricious reason to buy stock.

Carl E. Hathaway

ETHICS

There is no escaping the fact that the essence of an individual is his ethics. The more he seeks an ethical path, the more he mirrors the genius of his creator. To suggest that Americans and American business must submit to less than desirable practices in order to do business in foreign countries is totally inconsistent, absurd, and beneath comment. Ethics transcends circumstances.

Walter F. Beran

Uncertainty is the enemy of ethics. Many corporate employees have behaved improperly in the misguided belief that the front office wanted them to. If standards are not formulated systematically at the top, they will be formulated haphazardly and impulsively in the field.

John C. Biegler

The time has come for those of us in business to put our house in order . . . to restore the faith of Americans in the basic competence and purpose of business. And this requires a lot more than public-relations efforts.

Frank T. Cary

Men of business must not break their word twice.

Thomas Fuller

Businessmen's ethics are not any worse than those of the public as a whole. It's just that the businessman is more accountable than any other level of society and is much more likely to be caught in any dereliction of duty or responsibility.

C. Peter McColough

The public's confidence in business will not be revived by trying to make debating points. It will be restored only by a full awareness of the constantly changing standards of behavior expected of business leaders and by a genuine effort throughout the business community to adhere to them.

William S. Kanaga

Just as political liberty is threatened when men in power violate the spirit of our Constitutional freedoms, so is our free-enterprise system placed in jeopardy when a code of honesty and social responsibility is not honored by businessmen and women. If we remember to be wary of the principle that the end justifies the means, and that the economic benefit of our company is not a supreme good that overrides all other ethical considerations, we will be well on our way to helping restore the good name of our profession. The ethically right decision will ultimately prove to be the economically right decision as well. I don't believe that there has ever been a company that enjoyed a long period of success as a result of unethical or illegal practices.

Thomas A. Murphy

I question whether there can, over time, be such a thing as "corporate morality" or "corporate ethics," as distinct from that of the society of which it is a part and the people who make up that society. I believe there is only a corporate environment that responds to, and impacts upon, the individual behavior, morality and ethics of those who inhabit that environment.

Harold M. Williams

If business ethics are a luxury, or even a liability, it is only a matter of time before the system will be changed. In the long run, honesty is not only the best business policy, but the only one compatible with the free market and open competition. Business corruption is not only inefficient, but it destroys the marketplace.

Harold M. Williams

Nothing is illegal if a hundred businessmen decide to do it.

Andrew Young

EUROPEAN BUSINESSMEN

The characteristic of European businessmen as a class as distinguished from Americans is their complacency, their timidity, and their instinctive looking to each other and to the governments for protection against the rude shocks of the contemporary world. And the thing they fear most is price competition.

Clarence Randall

EXCELLENCE

What you want to do in business if you want to progress is to be like an asparagus patch, except you want to be a three-foot stalk of asparagus while everybody else is 18 inches.

Frank E. Hedrick

EXECUTIVE

A valuable executive must possess a willingness and ability to assume responsibility, a fair knowledge of his particular branch of business, and a nice understanding of business principles in general, also to be able to read and understand human nature. There is no phase of knowledge which anyone can safely dismiss as valueless.

Charles Cheney

The mark of a true executive is usually illegible.

Leo J. Farrell, Jr.

The executive exists to make sensible exceptions to general rules.

Elting E. Morison

The really top executive is a totally different breed of cat—a well-balanced human being who has imagination, a lot of common sense with it, who doesn't kid himself, put on a lot of airs or go off half-cocked and is persevering.

Walter H. Wheeler

Robot executives who cling to this-is-the-way-it's-always-been-done conformity are not only stifling their own careers but also precipitating a case of hardening of the arteries throughout industry.

Louis Wolfson

EXECUTIVE ABILITY

Executive ability is deciding quickly and getting someone else to do the work.

J. G. Pollard

EXECUTIVE BEHAVIOR

The short-term success in the 60s of the Jimmy Lings, the Saul Steinbergs, the Harry Figgies, the J. B. Fuquas, and even the Harold Geneens promoted a radical change in executive training and behavior. With their noses buried in numbers, executives have become risk-aversive and short-run oriented. They are building corporate hierarchies and bureaucracies that are every bit as lethargic, obstructive, and nonproductive as those in government about which people complain so bitterly. This obsession has shown up in declining competitiveness in world markets, a lack of innovation in new products, and shrinking R&D efforts.

Lewis H. Young

EXECUTIVE SALARY

The present salary structure among top corporate officers is archaic and completely inconsistent with our enterprise system. Executives are employees, not owners. [They] should get a bigger slice of the reward than those who are chosen from among many to run it for a little while.

John Z. De Lorean

EXPANSION

If you are going to develop a business, you had better not get too involved in details of an operation. You had better stay on the promotion side. I think that's why many small businessmen stay small. You know, it's like the garage mechanic who likes to stay under the car and the restaurant owner who never gets out of the kitchen.

Jay Van Andel

The key to success in business is understanding of the world about you and then making products to fit the needs of the times. A person who looks inward is bound to try to make the times try to fit his company's products.

Peter C. Vink

EXPERIENCE

Good judgment is the outcome of experience ... and experience is the outcome of bad judgment.

Vivien Fuchs

EXPERTS

Make three correct guesses consecutively and you will establish a reputation as an expert.

Laurence Peter

EXPLOITATION

The workingmen have been exploited all the way up and down the line by employers, landlords, everybody.

Henry Ford

F

FACTS

Facts that are not frankly faced have the habit of stabbing us in the back.

Sir Harold Bowden

Facts, as such, never settled anything. They are working tools only. It is the implications that can be drawn from facts that count, and to evaluate these requires wisdom and judgment.

Clarence B. Randall

If a businessman wants to have an impact, he better get his facts organized, go to Washington to present them and be prepared to take the heat if he's wrong.

Irving S. Shapiro

FAILURE

The only time you don't want to fail is the last time you try.

Charles F. Kettering

The freedom to fail may at times appear to be an overly painful solution—particularly to the firm going out of business. But business failures serve a higher public purpose. They are the means by which our economy discards obsolete or inefficient ways of doing business. In this way, the overall efficiency of our economy is improved. Business failures are not tragic events to be prevented; they are the signs of a healthy and productive economy.

William Proxmire

We are far more Communistic than the Russians when it comes to tolerating failure. When the men in Russia foul up, they are dismissed, sometimes losing their necks. But we protect those who fail and press them to the government bosom.

Hyman G. Rickover

FAITH

The greatest asset of a man, business, or a nation is faith.

Thomas J. Watson

FARMERS

There are plenty of farmers in the world who cannot read, but very few who cannot count.

David E. Lilienthal

FEDERAL AID

If the inefficient or mismanaged firm is insulated from the free-market pressures that other business firms must face, the result will be that scarce economic human resources will be squandered on enterprises whose activities do not meet the standards imposed by the marketplace—standards which have assured us of the efficiency on which our industrial supremacy has been built.

James L. Buckley

FEDERAL BUDGET

Virtually everything is under federal control except the federal budget.

Herman Talmadge

FEDERAL TRADE COMMISSION

I have never seen a group so anti-business. I would rather walk in with a problem to the Kremlin than I would to the Federal Trade Commission.

Robert D. Rowan

FINANCE

The selection of key executives who can properly manage one's assets and recognize what is achievable within the financial capability of the company is critical. It is vitally important for managers to understand financial limitations, to understand the parameters in which they are operating.

Edward S. Donnell

Finance is the art of passing currency from hand to hand until it finally disappears.

Robert W. Sarnoff

In a sense, the financial conflict is more bitter and ruthless than war itself; in war, friend and foe can be distinguished.

B. F. Winkelman

FINANCIERS

Those heroes of finance are like beads on a string—when one slips off, the rest follow.

Henrik Ibsen

FORECASTING

The executive of the future will be rated by his ability to anticipate his problems rather than to meet them as they come.

Howard Coonley

FOUNDATIONS

A large industrial organization that employs thousands of people is doing more good than many a foundation does.

J. Paul Getty

FOUNDERS

The great corporations of this country were not founded by ordinary people. They were founded by people with extraordinary energy, intelligence, ambition, aggressiveness. All those factors go into the primordial capitalist urge.

Daniel P. Moynihan

FRAUD

There are no new forms of financial fraud; in the last hundred years there have only been small variations of a few classic designs.

John Kenneth Galbraith

FREE CHOICE

The delusion that the consumer cannot trust his own free choice strikes at the very heart of our free competitive system. The system is founded on the conviction that in the long run the consumer is the best judge of his own welfare. The entire success of free enterprise can be traced to the vitality it gains by competitive striving to satisfy the discriminating consumer. To destroy the concept of consumer supremacy is to destroy free enterprise. If the consumer can be convinced that he really does not know what is good for him, then freedom leaves free enterprise.

James M. Roche

FREE ENTERPRISE

There is a common misconception about business and businessmen. We are often looked upon as the Establishment—whatever that is—dedicated to the preservation of the status quo. In fact, we are revolutionists. Business is in revolution. The concept of free enterprise is itself a very revolutionary idea. It is still not an accepted thought in most countries. It is not designed to preserve the status quo. It is designed for change. Successful corporate management concerns itself with forces of change. It creates, directs, and manages change.

William M. Batten

If free enterprise is to be saved, it must be shared. If it stops at the front office, it is doomed.

Wallace F. Bennett

We are privileged to live in a country where any man or woman is free to purchase an ownership interest in a great American business. This opportunity, this privilege, is one of the strongest elements in America's free enterprise system. It is part of our priceless heritage of equality and freedom. There is no stock exchange in Moscow.

G. Keith Funston

The free-enterprise system has gone to hell.

Lee Iacocca

One of the aspects of the free enterprise system is that you should be allowed to succeed, and you should also be allowed to fail.

Reginald Jones

If the spirit of business adventure is dulled, this country will cease to hold the foremost position in the world.

Andrew Mellon

The whole point of free enterprise—of capitalism—is vigorous, honest competition. Every corner cut, every bribe placed, every little cheating move by a businessman in pursuit of a quick plunder instead of honest profit is an outright attack on the real free-enterprise system.

William E. Simon

Our tradition of free enterprise is very limiting. In the past it has paid off in entrepreneurial vigor. But if we're moving into a deliberate industrialization policy, it will require capital investment induced and supported by government, with much more collaborative relations between government and business.

Albert T. Sommers

Men of colossal fortunes are in effect, if not in fact, trustees for the public.

Samuel Tilden

FREE MARKET

If business is going to continue to sell through the decades, it must also promote an understanding of what made those products possible, what is necessary to a free market, and what our free market means to the individual liberty of each of us, to be certain that the freedoms under which this nation was born and brought to this point shall endure in the future . . . for America is the product of our freedoms.

E. F. Hutton

FRIENDS

Our business is not just making beer; making friends is our business.

Adolphus Busch

FRIENDSHIP

A friendship founded on business is a good deal better than a business founded on friendship.

John D. Rockefeller

FRONTIER

There will always be a frontier where there is an open mind and a willing hand.

Charles F. Kettering

FUTURE

The real wave of the future is not Marxism, but free enterprise. It is not centralization, but decentralization. It is not the public sector, but the private sector. And, finally, it is not the nation-state but internation.

Arthur K. Watson

G

GAMBLE

You've got to gamble in this business, try new approaches. I'd rather go for the fast nickel than the slow buck. The carriage trade is not large enough to support the airlines of America. Anyone who tells you that the way to make money in this business is to charge higher prices to fewer passengers doesn't know his rear end from a hole in the ground.

Robert F. Six

GENERAL MOTORS

The history of General Motors over the past 50 years is far more important than the history of Switzerland or Holland.

Antony Jay

General Motors is not in the business of making cars. General Motors is in the business of making money.

Thomas A. Murphy

74

What is good for the General Motors is good for the country, and what is good for the country is good for the General Motors.

Charles E. Wilson

GETTING AHEAD

Our very business life is not to get ahead of others, but to get ahead of ourselves.

Thomas L. Monson

GETTING ALONG

The greatest ability in business is to get along with others and influence their actions. A chip on the shoulder is too heavy a piece of baggage to carry through life.

John Hancock

GIVING

Time and money spent in helping men to do more for themselves is far better than mere giving.

Henry Ford

Being very rich as far as I am concerned is having a margin. The margin is being able to give.

May Sarton

GLOBAL ECONOMY

American industry has no manifest destiny to be always first, always right, and always best. A world economy includes us, but we are no longer the majority stockholder.

David M. Roderick

GOLDEN RULE

Golden Rule principles are just as necessary for operating a business profitably as are trucks, typewriters, or twine.

James Cash Penney

If the Golden Rule is to be preached at all in these modern days, when so much of our life is devoted to business, it must be preached specially in its application to the conduct of business.

Ferdinand S. Schenck

GOOD

It's so much easier to do good than to be good.

B. C. Forbes

GOODWILL

A great asset of any business is goodwill. . . . Character, from which stems goodwill, is a quality of slow growth through performance.

W. Alton Jones

Goodwill is the one and only asset that competition cannot undersell nor destroy.

Marshall Field

GOSPEL OF WEALTH

The Gospel of Wealth advocates leaving free the operation of laws of accumulation.

Andrew Carnegie

GOVERNMENT

One of the things we have to be thankful for is that we don't get as much government as we pay for.

Charles F. Kettering

GOVERNMENT INTERFERENCE

I feel generally that we should have a minimum of government inter-
ference in business, but there does seem to be a need in some areas for
satisfactory spelling out of what the rules of the game should be, and
perhaps we just have to live with more government regulations.

H. Herman Browne

GOVERNMENT POWER

The natural consequence of a planned destruction of the economic
power of private corporations would be to transfer that power to government. It would not actually be destroyed. We would simply have big
government corporations. Today the people have recourse against
monopoly and inefficiency in private business. . . . There is no recourse
against government monopoly and inefficiency.

Charles E. Wilson

GOVERNMENT REGULATIONS

If private business should be supervised in the public interest, government, when it assumes a business role, is in equal need of supervision.

James A. Fulton

GREED

Maybe it's too easy to get greedy on Wall Street.

Donald T. Regan

Capital which overreaches for profits, labor which overreaches for wages, or a public which overreaches for bargains will destroy each other.

Owen D. Young

GROWTH

Some people grow in office; others merely swell.

Sir Richard Dobson

The overriding challenge with any company growth plan, whether for five or 15 years, is that it can only succeed if you are able to cope with the problems of today.

Donald B. Seibert

H

HAPPINESS

The formula for complete happiness is to be very busy with the unimportant.

A. Edward Newton

HARD WORK

Do it the hard way! Think ahead of your job. Then nothing in the world can keep the job ahead from reaching out for you. Do it better than it need be done. Next time doing it will be child's play. Let no one or anything stand between you and the difficult task, let nothing deny you this rich chance to gain strength by adversity, confidence by mastery, success by deserving it. Do it better each time. Do it better than anyone else can do it. I know this sounds old-fashioned. It is, but is has built the world.

Harlow H. Curtice

Hard work without talent is a shame, but talent without hard work is a tragedy.

Robert Half

HELP

A man is to go about his business as if he had not a friend in the world to help him in it.

Lord Halifax

HIRING

When you hire people who are smarter than you are, you prove you are smarter than they are.

R. H. Grant

HONESTY

The big thing is recognizing that honesty sells. There is no reason why honesty cannot be combined with the skills of persuasion.

William Bernbach

First honesty, then industry, then concentration.

Andrew Carnegie's motto

Businessmen are as honest as any given segment of society, and perhaps more honest than most. It's like motorcyclists. They are not all Hell's Angels. But there is a percent in business, and it varies from 2 percent to 10 percent, depending on your definition of dishonesty.

Malcolm S. Forbes

It is absurd for anyone to believe that an established businessman would deliberately cheat his customers. It costs so much money to introduce a new product or to build up a retail clientele, that only an idiot would risk losing that investment by going after a dishonest dollar or two. He might get that dollar once, but his customer will never come back. And there isn't a businessman in the country who can make a go of it on one-time patronage. He simply must have repeat business; and the only way he can get it is by delivering a good product or service at a fair price.

Thomas R. Shepard, Jr.

Business is more than 99.44% pure ... the charlatans, the malefactors, the quick buck artists represent no more than 1% of the business community, and all of industry must not be penalized for the sins of the few.

Maurice H. Stans

HONOR

No amount of ability is of the slightest avail without honor.

Andrew Carnegie

HOPE

In the factory we make cosmetics. In the store we sell hope.

Charles Revson

HUMAN DEVELOPMENT

The responsibility of business has expanded to the point where it can now be said that the business of business is human development. ... I am inclined to think that the corporation that is not in the business of human development may not be in any business.

William S. Vaughn

HUMAN RELATIONS

All great questions of politics and economics come down in the last analysis to the decisions and actions of individual men and women. They are questions of human relations, and we ought always to think about them in terms of men and women—the individual human beings who are involved in them. If we can get human relations on a proper basis, the statistics, finance, and all other complicated technical aspects of these questions will be easier to solve.

Thomas J. Watson

HYPE

If you hype something and it succeeds, you're a genius. If you hype it and it fails, then it's just a hype.

Neil Bogart

I

IDEAS

American business executives are quite narrow intellectually. Though not limited in intelligence, they tend to have tunnel vision because they spend up to 80 hours focusing on their specialized job in the corporation. They are committed to doing practical things, not to playing with ideas. You won't find them reading novels or plays. A lot of enormously bright executives do run around corporations with fantastic ideas, but they're not always heard, despite the fact that in the current rapidly changing environment firms must quickly come up with ideas that translate into new products.

Allan Cox

No idea is worth anything unless you have the guts to back it up.

Alonzo G. Decker, Sr.

Bigness alone is no assurance of success. Industry is ideas and innovation, and creative ideas can be achieved anywhere by anybody.

Thomas J. Watson

IDLENESS

I have often maintained that I possess a rare talent and a strong inclination to be a beachcomber. . . . If it were not for the demands made upon me by my business, I would provide living proof that a man can live quite happily for decades without ever doing any work.

John Paul Getty

IGNORANCE

If ignorance paid dividends, most Americans could make a fortune out of what they don't know about economics.

Luther Hodges

In modern business it is not the crook who is to be feared most, it's the honest man who doesn't know what he is doing.

Owen D. Young

INCENTIVES

Incentives are spurs that goad a man to do what he doesn't particularly like, to get something he does particularly want. They are rewards he voluntarily strives for.

Paul G. Hoffman

INCOME

The ideal income is a thousand dollars a day—and expenses.

Pierre Lorillard

If all sources of capital investment are dried up, the flow of all income may eventually cease.

Andrew Mellon

INCOME TAX

The hardest thing in the world to understand is the income tax.

Albert Einstein

The entire graduated income tax structure was created by Karl Marx.

Ronald Reagan

The income tax has made more liars out of the American people than golf has. When you make a tax form out on the level, you don't know, when it is through, if you are a crook or a martyr.

Will Rogers

INCOMPETENCE

A tragic error occurs when a man who is doing a job well is promoted to a position of incompetence. It is almost impossible to unpromote him.

Laurence J. Peter and Raymond Hull

INDECISION

Indecision is debilitating; it feeds upon itself; it is, one might say, almost habit-forming. Not only that, but it is contagious; it transmits itself to others.... Business is dependent on action. It cannot go forward by hesitation. Those in executive positions must fortify themselves with facts and accept responsibility for decisions based upon them. Often greater risk is involved in postponement than in making a wrong decision.

H. A. Hopf

INDUSTRIAL RELATIONS

Industrial relations are like sexual relations. It's better between two consenting parties.

Vic Feather

I have long been profoundly convinced that in the very nature of things, employees and employers are partners, not enemies; that their interests are common, not opposed; that in the long run the success of each is dependent upon the success of the other.

John D. Rockefeller, Jr.

INDUSTRY

The greatest menace to the life of an industry is industrial self-complacency.

David Sarnoff

INFLATION

Inflation is a hidden form of taxation which it is almost impossible to measure.

John Beckley

Inflation is one form of taxation that can be imposed without legislation.

Milton Friedman

No civilized country has ever voluntarily adopted the extreme philosophies of either fascism or communism, unless the middle class was first liquidated by inflation.

H. W. Prentis

Any inflation rate which is correctly and universally anticipated by the financial markets should have no effect at all on stock prices.

Ezra Solomon

We have a love-hate relationship. We hate inflation, but we love everything that causes it.

William Simon

INFORMATION

In the business world, an executive knows something about everything, a technician knows everything about something,—and the switchboard operator knows everything.

Harold Coffin

A businessman's judgment is no better than his information.

R. P. Lamont

Next to knowing all about your own business, the best thing to know is all about the other fellow's business.

John D. Rockefeller

Information about money has become almost as important as money itself.

Walter Wriston

INGENUITY

Never tell people how to do things. Tell them what to do and they will surprise you with their ingenuity.

George Patton

INNOVATION

Business has only two functions—marketing and innovation.

Peter Drucker

Replicate, don't innovate. . . . Someone else has gone and done your homework for you. They have taken the risk, the time and spent the dollars.

Steven W. Lapham

He who builds a better mousetrap these days runs into design difficulties, material shortages, patent-infringement suits, work stoppages, collusive bidding, discount discrimination—and taxes.

H. E. Martz

One of the things that is kind of shocking, or perhaps disappointing, is that most of the time innovations do not take place within the industry in which one would have expected them to take place.

Peter G. Peterson

INTEGRITY

Integrity is not some impractical notion dreamed up by naive do-gooders. Our integrity is the foundation for, the very basis of, our ability to do business.

A. W. Clausen

In the longer run, a reputation for integrity and honesty in all our dealings, wherever in the world they take place, is a critically important part of our competitive mix. The only sure guide is to do abroad what we are required to do at home.

James R. Greene

I would put integrity at the top among ingredients a businessman must have. Without it, a person doesn't have anything to build on.

Rawleigh Warner, Jr.

INTELLIGENCE

Intelligence is the effort to do the best you can at your particular job whether scrubbing a floor or running a corporation.

James C. Penney

INVENTION

It is the use to which a new invention is put, and not the invention itself, that determines its value to society.

David Sarnoff

INVESTMENT

Save for gold, jewels, works of art and perhaps good agricultural land, and a very few other things, there is no such thing as a permanent investment.

Bernard Baruch

There is nothing so disastrous as a rational investment in an irrational world.

John Maynard Keynes

Never invest your money in anything that eats or needs repairing.

Billy Rose

J

JOBS

There is no future in any job. The future lies in the man who holds the job.

George W. Crane

The right man can make a good job out of any job.

William Feather

JUDGMENT

When a top executive is selecting his key associates, there are only two qualities for which he should be willing to pay almost any price: taste and judgment. Almost everything else can be bought by the yard.

John W. Gardner

K

KEEPING AHEAD

Keeping a little ahead of conditions is one of the secrets of business; the trailer seldom goes far.

Charles M. Schwab

KEEPING WORD

In business a reputation for keeping absolutely to the letter and spirit of an agreement, even when it is unfavorable, is the most precious of assets, although it is not entered in the balance sheet.

Lord Chandos

KNOWLEDGE

Knowledge is the only instrument of production that is not subject to diminishing returns.

John Maurice Clark

The secret of business is to know something that nobody else knows.

Aristotle Onassis

L

LABOR

Labor is a highly changeable commodity—its quality deteriorates as its price mounts.

Wesley C. Mitchell

There is one thing needed to settle the labor question. We need employers with the courage to say No.

Clarence Randall

Much of the present difficulty in industrial relations arises from the fact that too many employers as well as too many legislators take the labor leader more seriously than he deserves to be taken, while taking the ordinary, everyday, middle-of-the-road wage-earner less seriously than he deserves to be taken.

Whiting Williams

LAISSEZ-FAIRE

America cannot survive half-rich, half-poor; half suburb, half slum. If the country wakes up it will not do so by way of laissez-faire.

Felix Rohatyn

LANGUAGE

Command of English, spoken or written, ranks at the top in business. Our main product is words, so a knowledge of their meaning and spelling and pronunciation is imperative.

William Feather

LAWS

The problem in America is not that the top 100 corporation presidents are violating the laws, though God knows they are; the problem is they're writing the laws.

Nicholas Johnson

LAWYERS

I don't want a lawyer to tell me what I cannot do. I hire him to tell me how to do what I want to do.

J. Pierpont Morgan

LEADERSHIP

The business executive must demonstrate unprecedented leadership—leadership that combines disciplined intellect and faith in the highest ideals. The business manager in a free society belongs to the people.

J. D. Batten

Skilled leaders share traits that elevate them above the majority of managers. While most managers concern themselves with doing things right, leaders focus on doing the right thing.

Warren Bennis

The question, "Who ought to be the boss?" is like asking "Who ought to be the tenor in the quartet?" Obviously, the man who can sing tenor.

Henry Ford

Many of the best potential business leaders in our country will never surface because they have been turned off on business in their youth.

E. L. Nicholson

Good leadership must be for the future, not for the past or present.

J. Arthur Urciuoli

There is no limit to what a man can do or where he can go, if he doesn't mind who gets the credit.

Robert Winship Woodruff

LENDING

It is better to give than to lend, and it costs about the same.

Sir Philip Gibbs

LIBERALISM

The real problem is that our so-called business leaders suffer from a lack of conviction, a lack of courage, and an obsession to be in tune with the trendy liberal notions of our time.

William E. Simon

LIFE

Life is a misery if you don't get more than you deserve.

Harry Oppenheimer

LISTENING

Good listeners generally make more sales than good talkers.

B. C. Holwick

Perhaps one of the major maladies of American business is its inability to listen, or better yet, to hear. Deafness to our kids, our customers, and, perhaps worst of all, to ourselves. We don't really hear what we are saying, yet we spend 60% of our time talking. But who's listening? Who really gives a damn?

Dean F. Thomas

LOBBYING

In the old days, businessmen thought if they made political contributions, that entitled them to something in Washington. They understand now that it doesn't buy them anything. If a businessman wants to have an impact, he better get his facts organized, go to Washington to present them, and be prepared to take the heat if he's wrong. We are not always right. But if we pull our facts together, and tell our story, we'll come out okay, because the facts of business are pretty good.

Irving S. Shapiro

LONG-RANGE PLANNING

There is some merit in not having to think about this quarter's earnings.

Jerry Jordan

LOSS

I've never been associated with a loss. I don't know what it feels like, and I don't want to find out.

Guy R. Odom

LUCK

I am a great believer in luck. The harder I work the more of it I seem to have.

F. L. Emerson

I think luck is the sense to recognize an opportunity and the ability to take advantage of it. Every one has had bad breaks, but everyone also has opportunities. The man who can smile at his breaks and grab his chances gets on.

Samuel Goldwyn

M

MACHINES

It's going to be a tough decision when the purchasing agent starts negotiating to buy the machine that's to replace him.

Dave Murray

There may be enough poetry in the whirr of our machines so that our machine age will become immortal.

Owen D. Young

MAN AND WOMAN

Practically all problems in the realm of judgment, in the realm of operating a business involving men and women . . . can be handled more efficiently by a man and a woman, in our estimation. The American people, if they had sense, would elect a man president and his wife as vice president.

Bruce and Beatrice Gould

MANAGEMENT

Businesses aren't run by geniuses. It is a matter of putting one foot after another in a logical fashion. The trick is in knowing what direction you want to go.

James R. Barker

It isn't enough today to think in terms of making a profit. It isn't enough today for a person to be skilled in management techniques. We need the person who has those skills to have a broader understanding of the role of business and the corporation in society.

William M. Batten

No man ever manages a legitimate business in this life without doing indirectly far more for others than he is trying to do for himself.

Henry Ward Beecher

Management is the marshaling of manpower, resources, and strategy in getting a job done.

M. E. Dimock

Management is not being brilliant. Management is being conscientious. Beware the genius manager. Management is doing a very few simple things and doing them well. [When] you put brilliant people into staff roles, don't let them ever make decisions because the secret of management is never to make a decision which ordinary human beings cannot carry out. Work is craftsmanship. Management is craftsmanship. Most of the time it is hard work to get a very few simple things across so that ordinary people can do it.

Peter F. Drucker

Management by objectives works if you know the objectives. Ninety percent of the time you don't.

Peter F. Drucker

Good management requires imagination to plan ahead, leadership by example, and being suspicious. Never think things are all they seem to be on the surface. Dig deeply for problem areas. Never be satisfied with mediocre performance. Also know your business intimately. Let other people go into details and then make them give you, in concise form, the recommendations that should guide your decisions. You need the courage to make decisions, right or wrong. It's essential that you have the ability to work with people and that you avoid company politics. There's no point in losing sleep once a decision is made. The time to lose sleep is before you make the decision. A wrong decision should never stop or delay your next one. The higher you go up the executive ladder, the fewer your bad decisions should be.

David Foster

I subscribe to the thought that most people have a finite reservoir of intellectual material to add to an enterprise and that when it's gone, it's gone. Then you have to put somebody else's reservoir to work.

John W. Hanley

The first myth of management is that it exists. The second myth is that success equals skill.

Robert Heller

Management authority today is derived more from personal qualities— possession of knowledge, skills, and values—than on ownership of capital or property.

John F. Mee

Many organizations are overmanaged. There is too much emphasis on management technique, as opposed to knowing and seeing what the heck is happening.

Henry Mintzberg

I am never satisfied unless I either do everything myself or personally superintend everything done even to an entry in the books. This I cannot help.

J. Pierpont Morgan

The secret of Japanese success is not technology, but a special way of managing people—a style that focuses a strong company philosophy, a distinct corporate culture, long-range staff development, and consensus decision-making.

William Ouchi

One must not lose those direct, sensitive, and trusting personal relationships which are the essentials of managing human beings. A [company] president must resist the solicitous urgings of his staff, who seek to conserve his time and energy by putting him into the traditional ivory tower. Once there, safely isolated from the functioning everyday realities that shape the lives of his employees, and the general public, he is well on the way to being neutralized. With the best will in this world, his staff will commandeer his appointment calendar and condense all adversity into easily swallowed capsules that won't upset his stomach. But without the continuous exposure to the challenge and the stimulation of contrary views, an executive will be ill-equipped to guide his company with strength and intelligence.

Herbert P. Patterson

The most important ingredient of good management is [employing] the kind of people who can develop and grow. The second is attempting to identify for these people the kind of opportunities they can expect.

Robert W. Reneker

Good management consists in showing average people how to do the work of superior people.

John D. Rockefeller

One man can't know the right answers to every problem, because he can't possibly have all the facts or all the considerations involved. That means, of course, that you have to pick people in whom you have confidence, who have gone through the hoops and have a lot of experience and have demonstrated good judgment. And then you have to give them the authority to make decisions. Sometimes you have to bite your tongue after they do make decisions and those decisions don't make sense. In those cases, you talk it out and try to learn why they went in certain directions. But you can't dictate—unless you want to make all the mistakes yourself.

H. I. Romnes

The most important thing I have ever learned about management is that the work must be done by other men.

Alfred P. Sloan, Jr.

The secret of successful management is to keep the five guys who hate you away from the five guys who haven't made up their minds.

Casey Stengel

Modern management is a continuous learning experience.

Robert D. Stuart, Jr.

Despite all of the educational and analytical infrastructure that has been built up around the alleged science of management, it still reduces itself simply to homework, common sense, and good communication.

Donn B. Tatum

When you get right down to it, one of the most important tasks of a manager is to eliminate his people's excuse for failure.

Robert Townsend

The primary purpose of good corporation management is to keep a company in business indefinitely.

Charles E. Wilson

MANAGEMENT AS ART

Management, never really a science, is becoming even more of an art form that seeks to reconcile what is desirable with what is doable.

George Weissman

MANAGER

A good manager is a man who isn't worried about his own career but rather the careers of those who work for him.

H. S. M. Burns

In an automated business the intuitive manager is obsolete. To be a manager in an automated business, of course, a man need not have a formal education, let alone a degree; indeed it would be hard to find an institution of learning where he could acquire today the education he needs to be a manager tomorrow. But, in the sense of being able to handle systematic knowledge, he will have to be highly educated.

Peter F. Drucker

The responsibility of the manager is to unleash the power of the organization.

Donald S. MacNaughton

The self-made manager in business is nearing the end of his road. Despite his own blind faith in the practical, he is already hiring professionally trained engineers, chemists, accountants, and hygienists. . . . He must himself turn to professional education, or surrender control to those who do.

Richard J. Walsh

MARKETPLACE

The marketplace is truly a regulatory agency—it could regulate most economic activities with speed, effectiveness, and freedom. The market system of regulation works. It has the power to discipline. It takes into account millions of transactions. It responds rapidly to unanticipated events and to secondary effects arising from its own regulatory action. This rapid response is in direct contrast to government regulation which slows change, inhibits new ideas, and frequently thwarts the use of invention.

J. Stanford Smith

MARKETS

One illusion is that you can industrialize a country by building factories. You don't. You industrialize it by building markets.

Paul G. Hoffmann

MATERIALISM

The cure for materialism is to have enough for everybody and to spare. When people are sure of having what they need they cease to think about it.

Henry Ford

MEDIA

Is the press anti-business? That question breeds another. How can the press be anti-business when the press is business and often big business at that? After all, we too face boards of directors, union leaders, EEOC, SEC, and stockholders. The tension between press and business in a relationship not quite so adversary as that which exists between press and government, is a healthy tension in a land of separated and balancing centers of power. Is the press anti-business? The answer is no. Is the press anti-dullness, anti-stuffiness, anti-corporate secrecy? The answer is yes. Is a probing, skeptical searching press coverage good for business? I think so. . . . Business and journalism share certain great values. We are both pro-opportunity, we are both pro-consumer, we are both pro-profit, and we are both pro-freedom.

Arthur Ochs Sulzberger

MEDIA RELATIONS

The businessman only wants two things said about his company—what he pays his public relations people to say and what he pays his advertising people to say. He doesn't like anybody ever to look above, beyond, or over that.

Don Hewitt

MEDIOCRITY

Only a mediocre person is always at his best.

Lawrence D. Bell

The business world worships mediocrity. Officially we revere free enterprise, initiative, and individuality. Unofficially we fear it.

George Lois

Only mediocrities rise to the top in a system that won't tolerate wave-making.

Laurence J. Peter

Sometimes I worry about being a success in a mediocre world.

Lily Tomlin

MEN AND WOMEN

As soon as a woman crosses the border into male territory, the nature of the professional combat changes.

François Giroud

MERCHANTS

The merchant in the 21st century will be more of a showman than he is today, more creative, more innovative, more concerned with how he presents his message to his customers. Rather than be a buyer-and-seller, rather than a department manager, tomorrow's merchant will be an impresario.

David L. Yunich

MERGERS AND ACQUISITIONS

The nation's most important industries were created by merger and acquisition. Without them we would probably . . . have been nationalized.

Ralph Ablon

Everybody is merging. It's the style. If you can't grow bigger, you have to get smaller. If you can't expand, suspend.

Sol Hurok

A [corporate] merger is an example of the timidity of American managers when faced with the choice between the adventure of capital investment and acquiring another company.

Robert Lekachman

MIDDLE AGE

Perhaps advertising people have come to the conclusion that middle age is obscene.

Charles F. Adams

MILLIONAIRE

The man who has a million dollars is as well off as if he were rich.

Attributed to John Jacob Astor III

In some ways, a millionaire just can't win. If he spends too freely, he is criticized for being extravagant and ostentatious. If, on the other hand, he lives quietly and thriftily, the same people who have criticized him for being profligate, will call him a miser.

J. Paul Getty

I don't want to be a millionaire. I just want to live like one.

Toots Shor

MINIMUM WAGE

The minimum wage has caused more misery and unemployment than anything since the great depression.

Ronald Reagan

MINORITY ENTERPRISE

We must make certain that minority enterprise is successful ... because ultimately its chief value is symbolic, and I believe we cannot afford the failure of this symbol.

K. A. Randall

MISTAKES

The business system is blessed with a built-in corrective, namely that one executive's mistakes become his competitor's assets.

Leo Cherne

Make sure you generate a reasonable number of mistakes. Too many executives are so afraid of error that they rigidify their organization with checks and counterchecks, discourage innovation, and, in the end, so structure themselves that they will miss the kind of offbeat opportunity that can send a company skyrocketing. So take a look at your record, and if you can come to the end of a year and see that you haven't made any mistakes, you just haven't tried everything you should have tried.

Fletcher L. Byrom

You will never stub your toe standing still. The faster you go, the more chance there is of stubbing your toe, but the more chance you have of getting somewhere.

Charles F. Kettering

There is nothing wrong with making mistakes. The only crime is to make the same mistake over and over again.

Paul F. Orreffice

Whenever I think, I make a mistake.

Roger Stevens

MISUNDERSTANDING

If one is rich and one's a woman, one can be quite misunderstood.

Katherine Graham

MONETARY POLICY

The history of great societies is invariably linked with the value of their money—the integrity of their financial systems. The debasement of currency eventually debases the political basis of society itself.

Alan Coleman

MONEY

Making money is fun, but it's pointless if you don't use the power it brings.

John Bentley

There is a current danger that money—especially in international affairs—is being regarded as an end rather than a means. The whole monetary system is an instrument for the achievement of purposes which have to do with the welfare of the people.

William Blackie

Bad money, even in small doses, is poison to the economic system.

W. Randolph Burgess

Money never starts an idea; it is the idea that starts the money.

W. J. Cameron

Where large sums of money are concerned, it is advisable to trust nobody.

Agatha Christie

If you can count your money, you don't have a billion dollars.

J. Paul Getty

Money is like manure. You have to spread it around or it smells.

J. Paul Getty

The only way to keep score in business is to add up how much money you make.

Harry Helmsley

Money is paper blood.

Attributed to Bob Hope

When a fellow says it ain't the money but the principle of the thing, it's the money.

Abe Martin (Frank McKinney Hubbard)

Money as money is nothing.

H. L. Hunt

Money doesn't interest me. But you must make money to go on building the business.

Rupert Murdoch

If a man runs after money, he's money-mad, if he keeps it, he's a capitalist; if he spends it, he's a playboy; if he doesn't get it, he's a ne'er-do-well; if he doesn't try to get it, he lacks ambition. If he gets it without working for it, he's a parasite; and if he accumulates it after a lifetime of hard work, people call him a fool who never got anything out of life.

Vic Oliver

After a certain point money is meaningless. It ceases to be the goal. The game is what counts.

Aristotle Onassis

The two most beautiful words in the English language are "Check Enclosed."

Dorothy Parker

It is true that money attracts, but much money repels.

Cynthia Ozick

I do everything for a reason. Most of the time the reason is money.

Suzy Parker

I believe the power to make money is a gift of God . . . to be developed and used to the best of our ability for the good of mankind.

John D. Rockefeller

I have ways of making money [others] know nothing of.

John D. Rockefeller

Starting out to make money is the greatest mistake in life. Do what you feel you have a flair for doing, and if you are good enough at it, the money will come.

Lord Rootes

The man who does not work for the love of work but only for money is not likely to make money nor to find much fun in life.

Charles M. Schwab

Money is always there but the pockets change; it is not in the same pockets after a change, and that is all there is to say about money.

Gertrude Stein

MONOPOLY

The fact that a business is large, efficient, and profitable does not mean that it takes advantage of the public.

Charles Clore

You and I have been taught that bigness and monopolies are bad—they are taboo in an enterprise-oriented economy. In spite of what our traditions tell us, both bigness and monopolies can have distinct and positive benefits to the consumer at home and to our efforts to enlarge our markets abroad.

Douglas Grymes

Monopoly is business at the end of its journey.

Henry Demarest Lloyd

MORALE

One uncooperative employee can sabotage an entire organization because bad spirit is more contagious than good spirit.

Robert Half

MULTINATIONALS

We appear to be moving in the direction of what will not really be multinational or international companies, but what we might call anational companies—companies without any nationality, belonging to all nationalities.

Carl A. Gerstacker

The multinational corporation's prime allegiance is to an orderly marketplace in which a growing number of customers are served with goods and services, employees are provided with jobs, taxes are paid, and shareholders receive dividends. Far more often than not, these interests coincide rather than conflict with those of the nation-state.

Harry Heltzer

The multinational corporation has done more to bring progress in developing countries than anything else that existed. All the government programs don't hold a candle to the real progress that comes when a multinational corporation goes into an undeveloped country and starts to produce something.

Charles H. Smith, Jr.

International commerce depends on at least rudimentary international law and commonly recognized rules of business conduct. Multinational corporations bring people together in shared tasks, promoting better understanding. Business may set the stage for helping us achieve the goal that eluded the 19th century socialists—the goal of lifting mankind above narrow nationalism into world citizenship.

Olcott D. Smith

I view multinational business as the spearhead of an irreversible drive toward a true world economy. It seeks the most efficient use of resources on a global scale. It encourages economic integration, generates new capital resources, and fosters the spread of useful technology and management knowhow.

Robert W. Sarnoff

An American company can no longer be happy in considering its foreign operations as so many puppet shows. There is no room in world business for the home office expert who flies into a country with a satchel full of directives and lots of advice. There is no place today for the attitude that what's good in America is good anywhere. For any of us to believe that

Americans have a monopoly on intelligence, business judgment, initiative, or inventiveness is more than naive—it's foolhardy and it is a direct denial of the very thing that made this country great: a competitive mixture of many talents, many cultures.

E. M. de Windt

MYTHS

We must not be hampered by yesterday's myths in concentrating on today's needs.

H. S. Geneen

N

NATIONALIZATION

There's more hidden nationalization in the United States than there probably is in the United Kingdom. We're living in a world where the mixed economy is here to stay, and there's no point in making a pig's breakfast of it. You might just as well make it a success.

Montague Finniston

NEEDS

What this country needs is a good five-cent nickel.

Franklin P. Adams

What this country needs is a good five-cent cigar.

Thomas Riley Marshall

NET

Net—the biggest word in the language of business.

Herbert Casson

NEW BUSINESS

There are six critical things you've got to have before you can get a company going. You need a concept of the enterprise in terms of the product or service you're going to deliver. You must have technical knowhow. You have to have physical resources. You have to have contacts. You have to have customer orders. [Finally], you have to have time.

Karl H. Vesper

NEW INDUSTRIES

If progress is to occur in the capitalist system, new industries must rise to displace the old ones. But the political order will almost inevitably support the old capital formations rather than the companies of the future, because the future has yet to manifest itself and, hence, has no voice. So when government grows, it tends to reinforce the power of the established economic configuration. The crucial conflict in every economy is between the established companies and the new ones.

George Gilder

NEW YORK STOCK EXCHANGE

What's good for the United States is good for the New York Stock Exchange. But what's good for the New York Stock Exchange might not be good for the United States.

William McChesney Martin, Jr.

I deal in a big floating crap game, one that is played every weekday in the richest and most exclusive casino in the world: the New York Stock Exchange.

Richard Ney

NO

When, against one's will, one is high-pressured into making a hurried decision, the best answer is always "No," because "No" is more easily changed to "Yes," than "Yes" is changed to "No."

Charles E. Nielson

O

OBJECTIVES

The core, the center, the essential starting point in managing is to have clear objectives. Management is making things happen and this means causing change. If you have not decided what you want to make happen, if what you want is unrealistic because it does not relate to the world as it is or will be, if it requires resources that you do not have or cannot create, if you do not make your plans known to those who have to carry them out, then you have not started.

C. T. Wyatt

OFFICES

Offices are a tremendous waste of time for chief executives and they create 60% of all the work that takes place in them. . . . In most cases, the boss is busy because he is in. He should be out where the rubber hits the road, working with people and watching them.

Lawrence A. Appleby

OIL

Oil is seldom found where it is most needed, and seldom needed where it is found.

L. E. J. Brouwer

Oil is a very complex business. It is not, unfortunately, very well understood by the public.

Otto Miller

OLD

If a thing is old, it is a sign that it was fit to live. Old families, old customs, old styles, survive because they are fit to survive. The guarantee of continuity is quality. Submerge the good in a flood of the new, and the good will come back to join the good which the new brings with it. Old-fashioned hospitality, old-fashioned politeness, old-fashioned honor in business had qualities of survival. These will come back.

Edward V. Rickenbacker

The most successful businessman is the one who holds onto the old just as long as it is good and grabs the new just as soon as it is better.

Robert P. Vanderpoel

OPEN MARKET

If the American people fail to achieve the political and social goals they choose for themselves for the remainder of this century, it'll be in large part because they have failed to strengthen and preserve the open market financial system which permits their implementation.

A. W. Clausen

OPPORTUNITY

In all human activities, particularly in all matters of business, times of stress and difficulty are seasons of opportunity when the seeds of progress are sown.

Thomas F. Woodlock

ORGANIZATION

Reorganization is the permanent condition of a vigorous organization.

Roy L. Ash

The only things that evolve by themselves in an organization are disorder, friction, and malperformance.

Peter Drucker

I believe that the best way to run an organization is to make sure that all of its work never gets done. Any time a boss tells me that a company gets all its work done, I figure it's a poorly run organization. You ought always to have more work chasing people than you have people chasing work.

Eli Ginzberg

I think that you organize companies best with very shallow rather than very deep organizations. The concepts of span of control, which are often articulated in textbooks, are no more than that—a textbook idea of what you do. One of the real problems in American industry, is that you get such incredible depth in management that the nature of a real problem never gets to the decisionmaker. Instead it gets diffused and interpreted by layers of management.

Edward G. Jordan

Take my assets—but leave me my organization and in five years I'll have it all back.

Alfred P. Sloan, Jr.

OVERDIVERSIFICATION

Several decades of overdiversification have brought the lesson home, and today there is a general tendency to make the whole enterprise greater than the sum of its divisions by exploiting the potential synergy of complementary products, shared technology, and common sources of supply.

Louis A. Allen

P

PACKAGING

If the packaging doesn't say "New" these days, it better say "Seven Cents Off."

Spencer Klaw

PARTNERS

Mr. Morgan buys his partners; I grow my own.

Andrew Carnegie

PAST

We must not be hampered by yesterday's myths in concentrating on today's needs.

Harold S. Geneen

PATENTS

The only thing that keeps us alive is our brilliance. The only thing protecting our brilliance is our patents.

Edwin Land

121

PATIENCE

Business is like fishing. You have to have patience.

Leopold D. Silberstein

The wayside of business is full of brilliant men who started out with a spurt, and lacked the stamina to finish. Their places were taken by patient and unshowy plodders who never knew when to quit.

J. R. Todd

PAYROLL

A man isn't a man until he has to meet a payroll.

Ivan Shaffer

PEOPLE

Good people will make any organizational structure work.

John G. Breen

Don't fall in love with a business. Fall in love with your people, but don't fall in love with a piece of steel or glass or plastic. Those things will come and go because of changes you can't control.

Douglas D. Danforth

To me, the most important element in management is the human being. So the first essential is to treat people with consideration.

Yoshiki Yamasaki

PERFORMANCE

Every individual in an organization should expect—and deserves—clearly defined communication of what is expected of him or her. Good performance and productivity should be rewarded with genuine appreciation and recognition. Well-ordered, but relaxed, discipline within an organization avoids looseness, idleness, and unnecessary arguments. And when it is understood that the element of human dignity is a genuine concern of the leaders of an organization, people develop the feeling that fairness, equity and understanding are the main ingredients of decision-making.

James P. McFarland

PERSONNEL

Few great men could pass Personnel.

Paul Goodman

The ability to deal with people is as purchasable a commodity as sugar or coffee. And I pay more for that ability than for any other under the sun.

John D. Rockefeller

PESSIMISM

One of the rarest phenomena is a really pessimistic businessman.

Miriam Beard

PIONEERING

Pioneering does not pay.

Andrew Carnegie

PLANNED OBSOLESCENCE

The changes in new models should be so novel and attractive as to create dissatisfaction with past models. Automobile design, of course, is not pure fashion, but the laws of Paris dressmakers have come to be a factor in the automobile industry.

Alfred P. Sloan, Jr.

PLANNING

Perfection of planning is a symptom of decay. During a period of exciting discovery or progress, there is no time to plan. The time for that comes later, when all the important work has been done.

C. Northcote Parkinson

Planning is but another word for the vision that sees a creative achievement before it is manifest. Control is but a name for direction.

James L. Pierce

Business planning must run in cycles of up to ten years or longer.

Nelson Rockefeller

PLUCK

Someone has said that the "p" is silent in the word "luck," but it belongs there neverthess.

James B. Hill

POOR

The best way to help the poor is not to become one of them.

Laing Hancock

I've never been poor, but only broke. Being poor is only a frame of mind. Being broke is a temporary phenomenon.

Michael Todd

POWER

The modern corporation is a political institution; its purpose is the creation of legitimate power in the industrial sphere.

Peter F. Drucker

Power means not having to raise your voice.

George Will

PREJUDICE

We've had some weird-looking people working for us. But if they do the job, we hire them. You can overcome all prejudice in the world if you make money for someone. They'll forgive your religion and everything.

William Bernbach

PRICE

There's no such thing as a free lunch.

Milton Friedman

If you pay peanuts, you get monkeys.

James Goldsmith

One man's price is another man's income.

Walter Heller

Of all the possible business strategies open to the firm, price strategy is the easiest [for competitors] to detect, to counteract, and hence to defeat.

Jesse W. Markham

If the price is too high, the consumer won't pay, and what can Congress possibly evolve that will work more surely than that?

Charles E. Wilson

PRICE FIXING

It is relatively easy to fix prices that are already fixed.

John Kenneth Galbraith

PRINCIPLES

We have always found that, if our principles were right, the area over which they were applied did not matter. Size is only a matter of the multiplication table.

Henry Ford

PRIORITIES

Most businessmen generally are so busy coping with immediate and piecemeal matters that there is a lamentable tendency to let the long run or future take care of itself. We often are so busy putting out fires, so to speak, that we find it difficult to do the planning that would prevent those fires from occurring in the first place. As a prominent educator has expressed it, Americans generally spend so much time on things that are urgent that we have none left to spend on those that are important.

Gustav Metzman

PRIVATE BUSINESS

Private business is the most effective resource allocator man has ever invented. For society to benefit from its dynamics and innovation, it is the social responsibility of business to make a profit; and it is the responsibility and opportunity of society to invent ways of applying business methods to meet the needs of man and of society. It must set incentives and constraints in such a way that profit is made doing the tasks society most needs in a manner society finds acceptable.

John Diebold

PRIVATE ENTERPRISE

The General Motors is as much a public enterprise as the U.S. Post Office ... wholly dependent on its survival during every second of its operations on a vast network of laws, protection, services, inducements, constraints, and coercions provided by innumerable governments, federal, state, local and foreign.

Robert Dahl

There is no such thing as a purely private enterprise, and we may perhaps say, also, that there is no such thing as a purely public enterprise. Certainly in the vast majority of the enterprises with which we are familiar, private and public activities are combined in varying proportions.

Richard T. Ely

Some 25 years ago, you could make a long distance call on a privately owned telephone system from San Francisco to New York for $28. For that same amount of money, you could send 1,376 letters. Today, you could make the same telephone call for two and a half dollars and for that amount you can send only 20 letters. So the government is investigating the Bell System!

Ronald Reagan

PROBABILITY

All business proceeds on beliefs, or judgments of probabilities, and not on certainties.

Charles W. Eliot

PROBLEM SOLVING

Any time you have a big company, you have a problem being as nimble as a smaller company, which is quicker to respond to changing conditions.

Edward Carlson

Problem-solving and constructive innovation are what business is all about.

Randall Meyer

The real problem is what to do with the problem solvers after the problems are solved.

Gay Talese

PRODUCTION

Production is not the application of tools to materials, but logic to work.

Peter Drucker

To regard money as the principal commodity of commerce and to deal in it as such and to regard the making of money as more important than producing goods—that is the central fallacy on which government and finance agree.

Henry Ford

PRODUCTIVITY

In the search for productivity the correct starting point is the marketing concept. Productivity is not an end in itself but one of the means to an end; and that end is consumer satisfaction.

Sir Donald Barron

Economic efficiency consists in making things that are worth more than they cost.

John Maurice Clark

A company cannot increase its productivity. People can.

Robert Half

The only way to attack poverty is to promote productivity and growth.

Norman Podhoretz

There is more to productivity than just quantity—quality is involved. We must restore the balance that has been lost between wages and productivity.

James M. Roche

PROFIT

Business without profit is not business any more than a pickle is a candy.

Charles F. Abbott

In business the earning of profit is something more than an incident of success. It is an essential condition of success; because the continued absence of profit spells failure.

Louis D. Brandeis

People who think only of profit in the next twenty years will not make any profit.

Paul Bougenaux

Businessmen commit a fraud when they say they're interested in anything but profit.

Jim Brooks

The essence of business success is not to make goods or to have a host of employees. The biggest word in the language of business is not gross, but net. To increase the net profits is efficiency.

Herbert Casson

It is a socialist idea that making profits is a vice; I consider the real vice is making losses.

Winston Churchill

Profitability is the sovereign criterion of the enterprise.

Peter Drucker

Food profits rise as you come closer to the table.

Claude Fuqua

Uninformed critics have so perverted the meaning of the word profits in the public mind that it has come to mean something like "undeserved income" or "the exploiter's unjust reward." Almost half of what are called profits are really the government's take from the operators of a business—the corporation's income tax. The part paid out in dividends is really "interest on equity"—a fee paid for the use of people's savings, essentially no different from interest paid on loans. And the remainder are profits reinvested in business—just as well called business savings or reinvested earnings. The advantages of calling these costs of operation by their right name is that people understand such things as taxes, interest, earnings and savings, because they are all part of the family budget.

Reginald H. Jones

When someone asked me, which do you put first, service or profits, I said naturally I put service first, but we can only serve by earning money.

Frederick R. Kappel

If you cannot make money on one dollar—if you do not coax one dollar to work hard for you, you won't know how to make money out of one hundred thousand dollars.

E. S. Kinnear

Many people seem honestly to believe that profit dollars are dollars which pour into the coffers of corporations and just lie there, not helping anyone, and which in turn can be taken away without hurting anyone. Yet there never was a profit dollar that didn't go to work, and promptly, whether by flowing out to the investors who reinvest it or by flowing through the business itself for plant and equipment or something else needed to improve or continue the business as a job-providing entity.

R. Heath Larry

The world is moving away from the doctrine that business should limit itself to classic profit-making. The definition of profit itself is changing. The meaning of cost is changing. For a corporation, costs even now include social objectives, equality of opportunity, management of natural resources, development of human resources, attainment of a just and stable society.

Carl H. Madden

There is nothing mutually exclusive about making a profit and serving the needs of society.

Charles B. McCoy

Profits are so basic to the continued existence of a private business that it is almost impossible to imagine a system of business priorities that does not place them near the top. That is why it is so common to hear profit described as the number one objective of every business. It is an oversimplified answer given to an unfair question. Actually, the objectives of a legitimate business are so closely intertwined and mutually dependent that it is impossible to break them off and arrange them in a neat row of easily distinguishable priorities. I think we must couple our answer with a clear statement that profit is neither the first nor the last of a responsible businessman's objectives—but it is central to his ability to meet any other business or business-related objective.

Thomas A. Murphy

The worst crime against working people is a company which fails to operate at a profit.

Samuel L. Gompers

Profit and social progress go together and in our free economy are inseparable.

James M. Roche

There's only one way a business can earn a profit, and that is to make a product a consumer wants to buy, produce it efficiently, provide good service and treat the consumer honestly and fairly.

James M. Roche

Profit today is a fighting word. Profits are the lifeblood of the economic system, the magic elixir upon which progress and all good things ultimately depend. But one man's lifeblood is another man's cancer.

Paul A. Samuelson

Profit is the ignition system of our economic engine.

Charles Sawyer

Profit is merely the index, the proof that production was for use. No one achieves a profit by producing things that are not used.

Gustav Stolper

There is no way profits can be too high. Profits are the fuel cells that energize our economy. Profits are the barometer of our economic climate, the standard by which we measure our economic well-being. To understand this is to recognize that the higher the profits, the more financial support for the better life.

Allen P. Stults

The pursuit of gain is the only way in which men can serve the needs of others whom they do not know.

Friedrich August von Hayek

Profits are part of the mechanism by which society decides what it wants to see produced.

Henry C. Wallich

Profit is absolutely necessary to a healthy enterprise because it is the price of the future. Absence of profit is literally the death of a company because it deprives a company of the future.

Henry Wendt

Restrain in regard to immediate profits has not only been our most profitable policy, it has been pretty nearly our only profitable one. It has been the inspiration of every distinctively successful method we have used.

Philip K. Wrigley

PROGRESS

You can't sit on the lid of progress. If you do, you will be blown to pieces.

Henry Kaiser

The price of progress is trouble.

Charles F. Kettering

It is harder to stay ahead than to get ahead.

Paul W. Lichfield

One of the fundamentals that has made America what it is today is our willingness to tear down and rebuild with the new and better, usually the bigger. To promote obsolescence is to accelerate progress.

Alfred P. Sloan

Our vast progress in transportation, past and future, is only a symbol of the progress that is possible by constantly striving toward new horizons in every human activity. Who can say what new horizons lie before us if we can but maintain the initiative and develop the imagination to penetrate them—new economic horizons, new horizons in the art of government, new social horizons, new horizons expanding in all direc- tions, to the end that greater degrees of wellbeing may be enjoyed by everyone, everywhere.

Alfred P. Sloan, Jr.

PROMOTERS

Promoters are just guys with two pieces of bread looking for a piece of cheese.

Evel Knievel

PROSPERITY

Here is a remarkable fact, that the masses of people in any country are prosperous and comfortable just in proportion as there are millionaires.

Andrew Carnegie

In the tiny space of twenty years, we have bred a whole generation of working Americans who take it for granted that they will never be out of a job or go a single year without a salary increase.

K. K. Duvall

The trick is to make sure you don't die waiting for prosperity to come.

Lee A. Iacocca

While it may be more than we can do to make businessmen folk heroes, it is at the very least essential that people see and feel the crucial link between the output of our industries and the kind of life we can enjoy.

Peter G. Peterson

PROTECTIONISM

Protectionism—whether by high tariff barriers or by the host of nontariff barriers we now see springing up—is no answer at all. It pushes us toward more inflation, it reduces the benefits of competition, it increases cost to the consumer, and it dims our image abroad and strains out international relations at the very time we are making an effort to improve them.

Daniel J. Haughton

PUBLIC INTEREST

Economic performance is no longer enough. Business is properly expected to act in the public interest as well as shareholders' interest.

Reginald Jones

If it is not in the interests of the public, it is not in the interests of business.

Joseph H. Defrees

PUBLIC NEEDS

The most effective way to encourage business to serve new public needs is to rely on market incentives. When the marketplace does not automatically translate a public need into a market demand, then government action may be required to change market conditions.

Henry Ford II

PUBLIC RELATIONS

Over the next 10 years, the public will demand justification for just about everything American industry is doing. If we have a point to make, then we had better start finding ways to make it.

B. R. Dorsey

I have found [public relations] to be the craft of arranging truths so that people will like you. Public relations specialists make flower arrangements of the facts, placing them so that the wilted and less attractive petals are hidden by sturdy blooms.

Alan Harrington

PUBLIC RESPONSIBILITY

I have a very deep conviction that there is more real responsibility in business leadership today than ever in the whole history of this country. There is a real recognition that the corporation has a kind of public responsibility. Banking and other business cannot be divorced from the ultimate best interests of the people. We cannot exist in a kind of vacuum or detachment from the well-being of the people.

Louis B. Lundberg

The price of power is responsibility for the public good.

Winthrop W. Aldrich

PUBLIC SERVICE

My motto is public service.

Al Capone

PUNCTUALITY

Punctuality is the soul of business.

Thomas Haliburton

PURCHASE

All purchases are born of dissatisfaction. No purchase of any product anywhere—impulsive or deliberate—is ever made unless the purchaser is first dissatisfied in his present state.

William M. Bryngselson

Q

QUALITY

The surest foundation of a manufacturing concern is quality. After that, and a long way after, comes cost.

Andrew Carnegie

Give them quality. That's the best kind of advertising.

Milton S. Hershey

QUESTION

If you can't stand the answer, don't ask the question.

T. A. Wilson

QUOTAS

Within us all there are wells of thought and dynamos of energy which are not suspected until emergencies arise. Then oftentimes we find that it is comparatively simple to double or treble our former capacities and to amaze ourselves by the results achieved. Quotas, when set up for us by others, are challenges which goad us on to surpass ourselves. The outstanding leaders of every age are those who set up their own quotas and constantly exceed them.

Thomas J. Watson

R

REAL ESTATE

More money has been made in real estate than in all industrial investments combined.

Andrew Carnegie

The best investment on earth is earth.

Louis Glickman

Real estate is the closest thing to the proverbial pot of gold.

Ada Louise Huxtable

What marijuana was to the sixties, real estate is to the eighties.

Ron Koslow

RECESSION

An economist's lag may be a politician's catastrophe.

George P. Schultz

RECOGNITION

Recognition for a job well done is high on the list of motivating influences for all people; more important in many instances than compensation itself.

John M. Wilson

REGULATION

The primary aim of all government regulation of the economic life of the community should not be to supplant the system of private economic enterprise, but to make it work.

Carl Becker

An unregulated economy is a jungle.

John C. Biegler

If we in business do not clean up our practices, the government will. We are up to our armpits with government regulations. Soon it will be over our heads.

A. W. Clausen

Regulation is the substitution of error for chance.

Fred J. Emery

The costs of government regulation fall ultimately on the same people who are benefited by regulation. The problem is not to abolish sin at any cost, but to find the best balance between benefits to people as citizens and costs to people as consumers.

Henry Ford II

Like the speed limits and stop signs we put on our highways and streets, [regulations] must be logical, workable, and economically feasible. We don't put stop signs in the middle of a busy highway, but we do put them in the path of American business.

Paul F. Orreffice

What is really wrong with over-regulation is not that business people don't agree with it, or that we find it burdensome and costly, but that in the long run its principal victim is the consumer. The fall guy is not the businessman; it is the shopper who pays for excessive regulation in higher prices, higher taxes, and reduced choices. Every regulation poses a threat to economic freedom, and its benefits must always be weighed against its costs, in terms of the average American's liberties as well as his pocketbook.

Thomas A. Murphy

I believe the root of the regulatory impulse is often arrogance. If you scratch an advocate of regulation, you are likely to find, very close to the surface, an arrogant impulse to substitute some personal vision of order for the apparent disorder of the marketplace. Practically, all of us are arrogant. Most businessmen are arrogant, particularly if they are chief executives. But, happily, there are checks against arrogance in business. The free market and the free consumer usually dictate to business. But when arrogance is embodied in public policy, there are no effective checks on it.

Robert T. Quittmeyer

During my tenure at the Treasury I watched with incredulity as businessmen ran to the government in every crisis, whining for handouts or protection from the very competition that has made this system so productive. . . . And, always, such gentlemen proclaimed their devotion to free enterprise and their opposition to the arbitrary intervention into our economic life by the state.

William Simon

RESEARCH

Research is a very costly business. Not more than one out of five research dollars ever pays off.

Crawford H. Greenewalt

Research is an organized method for keeping you reasonably dissatisfied with what you have.

Charles F. Kettering

Bankers regard research as most dangerous and a thing that makes banking hazardous to the rapid changes it brings about in industry.

Charles F. Kettering

Prosperity and obsolescence are absolutely tied together, and obsolescence makes prosperity. A research organization is the originator of obsolescence.

Charles F. Kettering

RETIREMENT

To continue much longer overwhelmed by business cares and with most of my thoughts wholly upon the way to make more money in the shortest time, must degrade me beyond hope of permanent recovery. I will resign business at thirty five.

Andrew Carnegie

A good retirement is about two weeks.

Alex Comfort

When a man retires and time is no longer a matter of urgent importance, his colleagues generally present him with a watch.

R. C. Sheriff

There is a limit to the contribution most senior people can make. If they have not made that contribution after six or seven years in a job, they are not likely to do so. On the other hand, if they have been effective, then they have already given their best effort. After that, it is time to bring in fresh minds to keep the company vital.

Edward R. Telling

I can't remember a day or week when I wasn't making decisions that would have an impact on this entire company. I never remember a period of relaxation when I wasn't concerned with some element of business. I do believe we ask more of an individual than we should when we ask him to bear the brunt of these decisions for an extended period of time. Ten years is long enough for a chairman or president.

Lynn Townsend

Nobody should be chief executive of anything for more than five or six years. By then, he's stale, bored and utterly dependent on his own cliches—though they may have been revolutionary ideas when he first brought them to the office.

Robert Townsend

RICH

If you want to know how rich you really are, find out what would be left of you tomorrow if you should lose every dollar you own tonight.

Wm. J. H. Boetcker

Poor people always lean forward when they speak because they want people to listen to them. Rich people can sit back.

Michael Caine

The man who dies rich is disgraced.

Andrew Carnegie

The rich get richer and the poor poorer.

Andrew Carnegie

Paying attention to simple little things that most men neglect makes a few men rich.

Henry Ford

There's no reason to be the richest man in the cemetery. You can't do any business from there.

Colonel Sanders

RISK

The worst thing that's happening in our country today is the overriding obsession for a riskless society. Safety, security . . . that's hell of a way to run a [business]. What's wrong with my losing money? Is that bad? That's my privilege, to make money and lose money. If I lose money, tough luck; if I make money, that's great. You should take your raps without being a crybaby.

Edward N. Cook

They tell me I often go out on a limb. Well, that's where I like to be.

Henry J. Kaiser

We shouldn't knock risk. The market and this country were built on risk.

Donald T. Regan

The higher the monkey climbs, the more he shows his ass.

Thomas Watson, Sr.

ROOM AT THE TOP

The most difficult part of getting to the top of the ladder is getting through the crowd at the bottom.

Arch Ward

ROUTINE

After you've done a thing for two years, you should look at it carefully. After five years, look at it with suspicion. After ten years throw it away and start all over.

Alfred E. Perlman

RULES

The executive exists to make sensible exceptions to general rules.

Elting E. Morison

RULES FOR BUSINESS SUCCESS

1. Carefully examine every detail of the business
2. Be prompt
3. Take time to consider and then decide quickly
4. Dare to go forward
5. Bear your trouble patiently
6. Maintain your integrity as a sacred thing
7. Never tell business lies
8. Make no useless acquaintances
9. Never try to appear as something more than you are
10. Pay your debts promptly
11. Learn how to risk your money at the right time
12. Shun strong liquor

13. Employ your time well
14. Do not reckon on chance
15. Be polite to everyone
16. Never be discouraged
17. Work hard

Baron Rothschild

S

SALARY

The salary of the chief executive of the large corporation is not a market reward for achievement. It is frequently in the nature of a warm personal gesture by the individual to himself.

J. K. Galbraith

SALES

The key to a sale is inequality of knowledge.

Deil O. Gustafson

If you were to list the one hundred most successful business organizations in America, I am sure you would find that the great majority of them are successful because they have employed unique or intensive sales methods.

W. Alton Jones

SALESMANSHIP

Successful salesmanship is 90% preparation and 10% presentation.

B. R. Canfield

A salesman, like a storage battery, is constantly discharging energy. Unless he is recharged at frequent intervals he soon runs dry. This is one of the greatest responsibilities of sales leadership.

R. H. Grant

To me, super salesmanship is not high pressure. It's living, 24 hours a day the work you are in, and naturally extends to everyone you contact.

Otto N. Hahn

Salesmanship consists of transferring a conviction by a seller to a buyer.

Paul G. Hoffman

Salesmen should bear in mind that more mature men who have reached a certain point in business buy rather than are sold. A real salesman does not attempt to sell his prospect but instead directs his efforts towards putting the prospects in a frame of mind so that he will be moved to action by a given set of facts.

Roy Howard

I think that American salesmanship can be a weapon more powerful than the atomic bomb.

Henry J. Kaiser

I am the world's worst salesman, therefore, I must make it easy for people to buy.

Frank W. Woolworth

The salesman who thinks that his first duty is selling is absolutely wrong. Selling is only one of the two important things a salesman is supposed to do—and it is not the more important of the two. The salesman's first duty is to make friends for his house.

Ellsworth M. Statler

SAVINGS

There is a certain Buddhistic calm that comes from having money in the bank.

Tom Robbins

SECURITIES

Like the cosmetics industry, the securities industry is engaged in selling illusions.

Paul A. Samuelson

SECURITY

The best means of security lie in a policy of constant innovation and expansion.

Herbert Croly

If money is your only hope for independence, you will never have it. The only real security that a man can have in this world is a reserve of knowledge, experience, and ability.

Henry Ford

We have completely gone overboard on security. Everything has to be secure, jobs, wages, hours—although the ultimate security is in jail, the slave labor camp, and the salt mine.

Cola Parker

SELF-MADE

There's nothing wrong with being a self-made man if you don't consider the job finished too soon.

John Mooney

SELLING

What we are selling are hopes and dreams, not frozen peas.

Michel C. Bergerac

There is no such thing as a soft sell and a hard sell. There is only smart sell and stupid sell.

Charles Brower

SENSITIVITY

The American business community is the most highly respected, highly regarded, indeed highly copied of any in the world. It has been hard-nosed. But when it has had to be, it has proved to be receptive, sensitive, and responsive. . . . The corporation that survives will be not only tough and hard-nosed, but also sensitive to the changes that are swirling about.

James M. Gavin

SERVICE

The vital force in business life is the honest desire to serve. Business is the science of service. He profits most who serves best. At the very bottom of the wish to render service must be honesty of purpose.

George Eberhard

The man who will use his skill and constructive imagination to see how much he can give for a dollar, instead of how little he can give for a dollar, is bound to succeed.

Henry Ford

I didn't go into business with the idea of making money. The opportunity for furnishing a service is more important than money as a motivating force for man. If you put quality first and service first, the money will take care of itself.

Joyce Hall

SHARING

Our most valuable possessions are those which can be shared without lessening—those which, when shared, multiply. Our least valuable possessions, on the other hand, are those which, when divided, are diminished.

William H. Danforth

SIMPLICITY

There is a master key to success with which no man can fail. Its name is simplicity. Simplicity, I mean, in the sense of reducing to the simplest possible terms every problem that besets us. Whenever I have met a business proposition which, after taking thought, I could not reduce to simplicity, I have left it alone.

Henri Deterding

SIZE

The size of General Motors is not the cause of its success, but the consequence of success.

James M. Roche

Excellence and size are fundamentally incompatible.

Robert C. Townsend

SLEEP

When I've had a rough day, before I go to sleep I ask myself if there is anything more I can do right now, and if there isn't, I sleep sound.

L. L. Colbert

SMALL

The next generation of whiz kids will be those who make big business efficiently smaller.

Anthony J. F. O'Reilly

SMALL BUSINESS

The more people who own little businesses of their own, the safer our country will be, and the better off its cities and towns, for the people who have a stake in their country and their community are its best citizens.

John Hancock

Small business is the biggest business of all.

J. E. Murray

SOCIAL AUDIT

The American businessman cannot consider his work done when he views the income balance in black at the end of an accounting period. It is necessary for him to trace the social incidence of the figures that appear in his statement and prove to the general public that his management has not only been profitable in the accounting sense but salutary in terms of popular benefits.

Colby M. Chester

It is unrealistic to contend that business must be free to pursue its own goals without reference to the broader needs and aims of the total society. All of us in business must recognize and accept the necessity for an expanded government role in our economic life. We must make the most of the situation by cooperating fully in setting the new ground rules.

Arjay Miller

I can foresee the day when, in addition to the annual financial statement, certified by independent accountants, corporations may be required to publish a social audit, similarly certified.

David Rockefeller

SOCIAL CHANGE

The problem in business is not competition but social change.

Laurence J. McGinley

SOCIAL ILLS

It should be made clear to the American people that business cannot and should not attempt to solve all of our present social ills. . . . It is no more reasonable to expect business to do everything than it is to expect government to be everything.

Arjay Miller

SOCIAL NEEDS

There is nothing mutually exclusive about making a profit and serving the needs of society. Personally, I have no doubt that the companies that will be the most profitable in the long run will be those that serve society best.

Charles B. McCoy

SOCIAL RESPONSIBILITY

The way to harness business to work with government in meeting social problems is to use the same system business uses in serving its customers: you make it terribly expensive to do things which hurt society and you make it very profitable to accomplish what society wants done. The thing that makes business so effective in responding to the changing requirements and demands of the consumer is not any special morality or capability on the part of its management, but the feedback control of the profit system. So the job of government is to set up incentives and constraints in such a way that business makes money doing what society most needs done.

John Diebold

To cater only to maximization of profits is to invite corporate doom. In this country, we've developed corporate enterprise by reason of the will of the people. The only way that we will continue to have the support of the people who enfranchised us is to perform in ways that are socially desirable.

Coy G. Eklund

Business leaders increasingly accept and act upon the belief that business can prosper and survive best through behavior compatible with the workings of the total life-support system, and that either social or ecological degradation of the environment in which business operates would not only impair but eventually bring down the profit-making corporation.

Coy G. Eklund

Real progress may lie in the loss of a company unable or unwilling to meet new standards of social responsibility.

John P. Fishwick

I believe the social responsibility of the corporation today is fundamentally the same as it has always been: to earn profits for shareholders by serving consumer wants with maximum efficiency. This is not the whole of the matter, but it is the heart of the matter.

Henry Ford II

Business does not meet its larger responsibilities to society by doing what is easy, convenient, and popular.

John J. Riccardo

Corporations must bear the cost of social responsibility or the consequences of evading it.

David Rockefeller

Who is competent to deal with the complex social problems of our time—the problems of poverty, race, population growth, environment, urban decay? Is there any reason to believe that government or labor or the universities are any more competent to deal with such problems than business? In these troubled times, the creativity and organizational skill, the energy, and resources of the business community are indispensable. It is, therefore, a challenge to business—indeed a responsibility—to harness its competence to the solution of our pressing social problems.

John D. Rockefeller III

The requirements for making a profit and the requirements for a socially responsible corporation are really interdependent and inseparable. The corporation's first duty is to gain the public's confidence in its products and services. When we act responsibly in areas outside the normal course of doing business, we reinforce the public's confidence in our company and its products. And that is good business.

Lynn A. Townsend

SOLVENCY

Solvency is entirely a matter of temperament and not of income.

Logan Pearsall Smith

SPECULATION

There is scarcely an instance of a man who has made a fortune by speculation and kept it.

Andrew Carnegie

You cannot stop speculation . . . in anything by process of law. Just as long as the value of property fluctuates, men will buy and sell with a hope of profit. There will always be speculation of some kind. If you throw it out of an organized exchange, you throw it out into the street.

Henry C. Emery

Inside every buy there is a sale screaming to get out.

Robert Heller

If there were no bad speculations, there could be no good investments. If there were no wild ventures, there would be no brilliantly successful enterprises.

F. W. Hirst

I never gamble.

J. Pierpont Morgan

I claim that this country has been built by speculation, and further progress must be made in that line.

Richard Whitney

SPENDING

More people should learn to tell their dollars where to go instead of asking them where they went.

Roger Babson

STANDARDS

If standards are not formulated systematically at the top, they will be formulated haphazardly and impulsively in the field.

John C. Biegler

STATISTICS

It does not follow that because something can be counted it therefore should be counted.

Harold L. Enarson

STEWARDSHIP

The surplus wealth we have gained to some extent at least belongs to our fellow beings; we are only the temporary custodians of our fortunes, and let us be careful that no just complaint can be made against our stewardship.

Jacob H. Schiff

STOCK MARKET

Repeatedly in my market operations I have sold a stock while it was rising—and that has been one reason why I have held on to my fortune.

Bernard Baruch

There is no such thing as an innocent purchaser of stocks.

Louis D. Brandeis

The stock market acts as a reservoir and distributor of capital with something of the same efficiency with which a series of well-regulated locks and dams operates to equalize the irregular current of a river.

Charles A. Conant

If you don't know who you are, the stock market is an expensive place to find out.

George Goodman

The most certain mechanism by which men can survive while other men are going under is to be on the side of the disaster. In a plague, corner the market in coffins, in an earthquake, invest in concrete; in a war, sell guns or oil; in a depression, sell short.

Kenneth Lamott

Bulls and bears aren't responsible for as many stock losses as bum steers.

Olin Miller

The stock market has a history of moving to irrational extremes because, on a short-term basis, stock prices are often more a reflection of fear, greed, or other psychological factors than of business and monetary fundamentals.

Joseph L. Oppenheimer

The stock market represents the simplest, most orderly, and most effective way to put savings to work. People who use stocks in a consistent and thoughtful way can't help but prosper over the long pull because they are betting on the future growth of the country—and that is as sound a bet as I know how to make.

Thomas R. Reeves

STOCKS

Stocks do not move unless they are pushed.

S. Jay Levin

You don't buy a stock because it has real value. You buy it because you feel there is always a greater fool down the street ready to pay more than you paid.

Donald J. Stocking

STRESS

People ask me, "How can you take all the pressure on a job like this?" And I think I can answer for all chief executives: We love it. Any man in the top spot will say things like: "It's tough—tough and hard." But boy, take that pressure away from them and they burst.

Fred J. Borch

SUBORDINATES

There are two kinds of people who never amount to much: those who cannot do what they are told and those who can do nothing else.

Cyrus H. K. Curtis

SUBSIDY

One of my saddest experiences has been to watch as some of our business leaders act perfectly contented when profits are rolling in but the moment there's a cloud on the economic horizon, they come running to Washington looking for a subsidy.

William E. Simon

SUCCESS

If at first you don't succeed you're running about average.

M. H. Alderson

The toughest thing about success is that you've got to keep on being a success. Talent is only a starting point in business. You've got to keep working that talent.

Irving Berlin

At sometime in the life cycle of virtually every organization, its ability to succeed in spite of itself runs out.

Richard H. Brien

The successful businessman sometimes makes his money by ability and experience, but he generally makes it by mistake.

G. K. Chesterton

What is the recipe for successful achievement? To my mind there are just four essential ingredients: Choose a career you love ... Give it the best there is in you ... Seize your opportunities ... And be a member of the team. In no country but America, I believe, is it possible to fulfill all four of these requirements.

Benjamin F. Fairless

Coming together is a beginning; keeping together is progress; working together is success.

Henry Ford

Every man should make up his mind that if he expects to succeed he must give an honest return for the other man's dollar.

E. H. Harriman

The price for success is so steep that most people give up. It may mean working 20 hours a day, neglecting family and friends. It may mean years and years of living on airplanes, sleeping in strange motels night after night, putting up with poor food in bad restaurants, always thinking about your wife and kids, missing them but seldom seeing them. The loneliness, the discomfort, the sweat and tears and sacrifice all become an emotional burden that grows heavier and heavier as you keep climbing the mountain toward business success.

Eugene Klein

Success is that old ABC—ability, breaks, and courage.

Charles Luckman

In many businesses, today will end at five o'clock. Those bent on success, however, make today last from yesterday right through tomorrow.

Lawrence H. Martin

Every successful enterprise requires three men—a dreamer, a businessman, and a son-of-a-bitch.

Peter McArthur

When a man blames others for his failures, it's a good idea to credit others with his successes.

Howard W. Newton

Financial success improves people who are good and debases people who are bad.

John Osborne

I can give you a six-word formula for success—"Think things through—then follow through."

Edward Rickenbacker

If you want to succeed you should strike out on new paths rather than travel the worn paths of accepted success.

John D. Rockefeller

Success or failure in business is caused more by mental attitude even than by mental capacities.

Walter Dill Scott

It is not enough to succeed. Others must fail.

Gore Vidal

The key to success in business is understanding the world about you and then making products to fit the needs of the times. A person who looks inward is bound to try to make the times try to fit his company's products.

Pieter C. Vink

Whenever an individual or a business decides that success has been attained, progress stops.

Thomas J. Watson

SUCCESSION

The crucial part of any executive's job is to pick the right successor. The moment a new chairman sits down as the desk, his first thought should be how best to plan for future leadership.

Edward R. Telling

SUPERIORS

Americans do not want much power distance between superiors and subordinates.

William Gordon

SUPERVISION

There comes a point in any organization where too much supervision means that supervisors spend too much time writing memorandums to one another, making needless telephone calls to one another, and the like, with no more productive work being accomplished in the aggregate, and possibly even less. We must strike the correct balance between too much supervision and too little supervision.

Gustav Metzman

T

TAKE-HOME PAY

Maybe they call it take-home pay because there is no other place you can afford to go with it.

Franklin P. Jones

TAKEOVERS

The takeover syndrome is not likely to reverse itself, but its character may change. Some of the targets of takeovers may be conglomerates that have failed to do a good job with the properties they have acquired. They may be devoured by the same techniques they used to acquire other companies.

Leon Levy

TASTE

Good taste is good business.

Joyce Hall

TAXES

Business organizations, by their very nature, are merely tax collectors, not taxpayers. Taxes are just another item of cost.

John Beckley

Why shouldn't the American people take half my money from me? I took all of it from them.

Edward A. Filene

Progressive taxation of income and inheritance is a mode of disguised expropriation of successful capitalists and entrepreneurs.

Ludwig von Mises

Anybody has a right to evade taxes if he can get away with it. No citizen has a moral obligation to assist in maintaining the government.

J. P. Morgan

The tax laws of the United States have been written to make private enterprise unworkable.

Sumner H. Slichter

TEAMWORK

No matter how much work a man can do, no matter how engaging his personality may be, he will not advance far in business if he cannot work through others.

John Craig

In business, as most of it is constituted today, a man becomes valuable only as he recognizes the relation of his work to that of all his associates. One worker more or less makes little difference to most big organizations, and any man may be replaced. It is the cumulative effort that counts.

W. Alton Jones

In order to succeed in any venture, you don't need a team of people, you need the right man to head up the effort and then he'll develop his own team.

John H. Williams

TECHNOLOGY

America's technology has turned in upon itself; its corporate form makes it the servant of profits, not the servant of human needs.

Alice Embree

The economic and technological triumphs of the past few years have not solved as many problems as we thought they would, and, in fact, have brought us new problems we did not foresee.

Henry Ford II

TELEVISION

A stake in commercial television is the equivalent of having a license to print money.

Lord Thomson of Fleet

TEMPER

A man who cannot command his temper should not think of being a man of business.

Lord Chesterfield

THINKING

Thinking is the hardest work there is, which is the probable reason why so few engage in it.

Henry Ford

Thinking is the one thing no one has ever been able to tax.

Charles F. Kettering

THOUGHT

Thought, not money, is the real business capital, and if you know absolutely that what you are doing is right, then you are bound to accomplish it in due season.

Harvey S. Firestone

THRIFT

Thrift is the great fortune-maker. It draws the line between the savage and the civilized man.

Andrew Carnegie

TICKER TAPE

There is nothing like the ticker tape except a woman—nothing that promises, hour after hour, day after day, such sudden developments, nothing that disappoints so often or occasionally fulfills with such unbelievable and passionate magnificence.

Walter Knowleton Gutman

TOMORROW

The first thing to do to attain tomorrow is always to be sloughing off yesterday.

Thomas R. Horton

One of the greatest labor-saving inventions of today is tomorrow.

Vincent T. Foss

TOP MANAGEMENT

There's plenty of room at the top, but there's no room to sit down.

Helen Downey

TRADE

What is needed is a clearcut economic trade policy representing a union of thought, effort, and purpose between private enterprise and government that will best serve the interests of the nation. Such a policy should neither promulgate the myth of free trade nor advocate the smothering cloak of protectionism, but instead grant to American industry the chance to compete on a fair and equitable basis.

R. F. Barker

TRAINING

Management is now where the medical profession was when it decided that working in a drugstore was not sufficient training to become a doctor.

Lawrence Appleby

TROUBLE

Trouble is only opportunity in work clothes.

Henry J. Kaiser

TRUTH

Truth in advertising and in business is neither likely nor entirely possible.

Neal W. O'Connor

Honesty in advertising is a matter of pragmatics as well as morality. I can't think of a faster way to ruin a product than with advertising that's not truthful.

Joan Seidman

U

UNCERTAINTY

Our business system is marvelously adaptive. But the one thing that it cannot handle is continual uncertainty. Business will play by the rules of the game—whatever they are—as long as those rules are not changed halfway through the game.

Richard L. Lesher

UNEMPLOYMENT INSURANCE

Unemployment insurance is a prepaid vacation plan for freeloaders.

Ronald Reagan

UNIONS

It is the mission of the trade unions to reform capitalism.

Thomas Burns

Labor unions are the worst thing that ever struck the earth because they take away a man's independence.

Henry Ford

It is management's problem to learn how to live with the union rather than try to undermine it or fight it. You don't have to agree to everything the union demands, but you do have to recognize that unions have a place in modern industry.

Ira Mosher

Unions are simply more or less complete monopolies and possess the same ability to raise prices as does any sellers' monopoly.

Sumner H. Slichter

As long as there are big corporations, there will be big unions. The economic power of big business will be matched by the economic power of the big unions.

Margaret Chase Smith

URGENCY

The more unpleasant it is, the more urgent it is.

J. D. Stewart

W

WAGES

It is not the employer who pays wages—he only handles the money. It is the product that pays wages.

Henry Ford

Men lose out when women get low wages, for the reason that low wages for women undercut the standards for men too.

Mary Agnes Hamilton

WALL STREET

There are only two emotions in Wall Street: fear and greed.

William M. Lefevre

I am not in Wall Street for my health.

J. P. Morgan

Many Wall Street firms have what they call a capital structure, but which more closely resembles a scaffold.

Donald T. Regan

In Wall Street the only thing that's hard to explain is—next week.

Louis Rukeyser

You've got more crooks in Wall Street than in any other industry I've ever seen.

Louis Wolfson

WANT

The problem of abolishing want is not a problem in division, as the politicians so often aver; it is a problem in multiplication.

Henry M. Wriston

WANTS

Human wants are never satisfied.

J. Willard Marriott

WASTE

Some have an idea that the reason we in this country discard things so easily is because we have so much. The facts are exactly the opposite—the reason we have so much is simply because we discard things so readily. We replace the old in return for something that will serve us better.

Alfred P. Sloan, Jr.

All organizations are at least 50% waste—wasted people, wasted effort, wasted space and wasted time.

Robert Townsend

WEALTH

You can only drink thirty or forty glasses of beer a day, no matter how rich you are.

Adolphus A. Busch

The only noble use of surplus wealth is this: That it be regarded as a sacred trust to be administered by its possessor into whose hands it flows, for the highest good of the people.

Andrew Carnegie

The eminently successful man should be aware of the tendency of wealth to chill and isolate.

Otto H. Kahn

You are affluent when you buy what you want, do what you wish, and don't give a thought to what it costs.

J. Pierpont Morgan

I was born into it and there was nothing I could do about it. It was there like air or food or any other element.

John D. Rockefeller, Jr.

I can't help from making money, that's all.

Helena Rubenstein

The advantages of wealth are greatly exaggerated.

Leland Stanford

Beware of inherited wealth. The job of getting is better than spending.

Robert R. Young

WILLINGNESS

In business, willingness is just as important as ability.

Paul G. Hoffman

WINNING

You win some, you lose some, and some are rained out.

Henry Ford II

WOMEN

In a society in which money determines value, women are a group who work outside the money economy.

Margaret Benston

Women are operating in institutions created by men, and that is like being in another culture, a foreign country. There are some male behavioral patterns that women have not grown up with. It is hard for women to become part of the informal power networks in the company. Men are in them naturally, and the information and reinforcement they receive are essential to moving ahead. Women are thus held to a difficult standard. They are expected to strike exactly the right balance between being aggressive and tough-minded on the one hand and being feminine on the other. And they find it's often a no-win situation.

Barbara H. Franklin

You cannot decree women to be sexually free when they are not economically free.

Shere Hite

The woman who climbs to a high post and then wants everybody to know how important she is, is the worst enemy of her own sex.

Mrs. Claire Giannini Hoffman

Men always try to keep women out of business so they won't find out how much fun it really is.

Vivien Kellems

To be successful a woman has to be much better at her job than a man.

Golda Meir

As economic affluence increased with the growth of the new industrialism and expansion of trade, women's worth declined as producers and increased as consumers.

Alice Rossi

The average secretary in the U.S. is better educated than the average boss.

Gloria Steinem

WORK

We continue to overlook the fact that work has become a leisure activity.

Mark Abrams

There are two things needed in these days: first, for rich men to find out how poor men live; and second, for poor men to know how rich men work.

E. Atkinson

Whatever task you undertake, do it with all your heart and soul. Always be courteous, never be discouraged. Beware of him who promises something for nothing. Do not blame anybody for your mistakes and failures. Do not look for approval except the consciousness of doing your best.

Bernard Baruch

The workplace is an island of authoritarianism.

Irving Bluestone

If not controlled, work will flow to the competent man until he submerges.

Charles Boyle

So much of what we call management consists in making it difficult for people to work.

Peter Drucker

In the tiny space of 20 years, we have bred a whole generation of working Americans who take it for granted that they will never be out of a job or go a single year without salary increase.

K. K. DuVall

I've always worried about people who are willing to work for nothing. Sometimes, that's all you get out of them—nothing.

Sam Ervin

Failures are few among people who have found a work they like enough to do it well. You invest money in your work; invest love in it too. Like your work. Like the materials and the tools with which you work. Like the people with whom you work. Like the place where you work. It pays well.

Clarence E. Flynn

The average worker wants a job in which he does not have to put forth much physical exertion—above all, he wants a job in which he does not have to think.

Henry Ford

Life is work, and everything you do is so much more experience. And whatever you do you must either use or lose.

Henry Ford

The world is full of willing people; some willing to work, the rest willing to let them.

Robert Frost

Work is a form of nervousness.

Don Herold

I have less religion, less family, less quality of life, less a lot of things because I am willing to make a commitment to participate in running a company.

Luther H. Hodges, Jr.

Most people like hard work. Particularly when they are paying for it.

Franklin P. Jones

When your work speaks for itself, don't interrupt.

Henry Kaiser

There has never been any 30-hour week for men who had anything to do.

Charles F. Kettering

If you have a job that needs to be done, give it to a busy man.

Robert E. Kirby

Opportunities are usually disguised as hard work, so most people don't recognize them.

Ann Landers

Don't tell me how hard you work. Tell me how much you get done.

James Ling

Work expands so as to fill the time available for its completion. General recognition of this fact is shown in the proverbial phrase "It's the busiest man who has time to spare."

C. Northcote Parkinson

Work is accomplished by those employees who have not yet reached their level of incompetence.

Laurence J. Peter

No one ever got very far by working a 40-hour week. Most of the notable people I know are trying to manage a 40-hour day.

Channing Pollock

Whatever you do, if you do it hard enough, you'll enjoy it. The important thing is to work and work hard.

David Rockefeller

Don't be misled into believing that somehow the world owes you a living. The boy who believes that his parents, or the government, or anyone else owes him his livelihood and that he can collect it without labor will wake up one day and find himself working for another boy who did not have that belief and, therefore, earned the right to have others work for him.

David Sarnoff

Even for the neurotic executive—as for everyone else—work has a great therapeutic value; it's generally his last refuge, and deterioration there marks the final collapse of the man; his marriage, his social life and the outside interests—all have suffered beforehand.

Richard Austin Smith

I have succeeded in getting my actual work down to thirty minutes a day. That leaves me eighteen hours for engineering.

Charles Steinmetz

Workmen will apply themselves better to their work when they can see directly that they are getting somewhere.

Charles E. Wilson

WORKER

A man can be as truly a saint in a factory as in a monastery, and there is as much need of him in the one as in the other.

Robert J. McCracken

The world is moved not only by the mighty shoves of the heroes but also by the aggregate of the tiny pushes of each honest worker.

Frank C. Ross

The most tragic error of management has been to thoughtlessly assume that the workman is a different sort of person.

Denton K. Swartwout

There are many millions of workers who actually, honest-to-God, like their jobs and are proud of their skills. Most people enjoy going to work in the morning. They find their tasks interesting—even challenging. The cadence of the job has a healthy rhythm. Their rewards are tangible and satisfying.

Robert F. Six

WORK ETHIC

When comfortable people, relaxing at their country clubs, deplore the alleged decline of the work ethic, they should not be taken too seriously. After all, if hard work were such a wonderful thing, surely the rich would have kept it all to themselves.

Lane Kirkland

WORKING CLASS

I can hire one-half of the working class to kill the other half.

Jay Gould

WORLD LEADERSHIP

The United States must take the lead in developing world peace through world business. No other nation or group of nations has demonstrated the benefits of free enterprise more graphically. We are the most advanced, most affluent and most well-endowed nation on earth. I don't hesitate for a moment to state that we arrived at this position through the steady and fruitful pursuit of profits.

E. M. de Windt

WORRY

The reason why worry kills more people than work is that more people worry than work.

Robert Frost

X

X-FACTOR

The X-factor is that little something special that you find in the human qualities of a corporation. You can have the finest plants and the best raw materials and all of the finances that you can possibly want; but if you don't have the proper human beings to manage so that they will produce income and goods of a quality that can be sold to customers at a profit, you don't have that X-factor, the human factor. You have nothing.

Thomas F. Patton

Y

YESMEN

I don't want any yes-men around me. I want everyone telling me the truth—even though it costs him his job.

Samuel Goldwyn

YOUTH

The fact is that much of the so-called youth advertising is not even understood by the youths themselves. The average youth of today is sophisticated, better educated than ever before in our history. They have learned to develop and enjoy diversity. There are times for swinging and times for serious planning of their lives and careers. And yet advertising too often makes the mistake of assuming that a swinger is a swinger—and nothing else at any time. In my opinion, such an attitude is an insult to the intelligence of the young adult.

Edward N. Cole

In the challenging days of tomorrow, business achievement will come to be measured by the new criterion of how effectively it solves the multiple problems of an expanding and complex civilization. But if business leaders are to be successful in this new endeavor, they will depend, to an enormous degree, upon attracting to their ranks the most talented of our concerned young men and women. The rub, of course, is that these bright young people are apt to disturb us most, because they vigorously challenge the status quo. Nevertheless, they are precisely the ones that we in business must enlist in our cause, for they possess that flexibility of mind which, particularly in the young, produces challenging and disturbing, but often worthwhile, new thoughts and programs.

Charles W. V. Meares

Unless we make our youth cognizant of the role of business in society, we have lost our youth. And when you lose your youth, you lose your future.

Edgar B. Speer

Z

ZEAL

Morale is the state of mind. It is steadfastness and courage and hope. It is confidence and zeal and loyalty. It is *élan, esprit de corps*, and determination.

George Catlett Marshall

NAME INDEX

A

B

S

T

U

V

W